Airbrush Technique

Airbrush Technique

Beyond Photography

C. Michael Mette

TACO

CONTENTS

Anyone who has been following the scene of international illustrators closely will have noticed that there has been a change of attitude towards the airbrush. There used to be a time when this tool was used only occasionally for photo retouching, as a kind of secret weapon, while in the world of art it was regarded with contempt. In recent years, however, it has developed into an all-purpose tool for those who are interested in "photographic realism".

As a result, quite a number of worthwhile works were created. But some of them were of inferior quality. For a long time those who were interested in airbrush artwork could really only learn through trial and error, i.e. by teaching themselves. And many artists put their works on the market too quickly. When the first books were published on this subject, it was particularly Japanese authors, illustrators and publishers who were foremost in the field, and there was a sudden surge of ardent enthusiasm among those who took an interest in this art form, with new information being snatched up immediately.

After the first gust of euphoria had calmed down a little, people became more discriminating and stopped buying up anything without regard to quality for there was now a demand for detailed information, especially intelligible information – after all, who could read Japanese?

Soon books were being written both in England, where the airbrush had been invented, and also in the States, the land of unlimited opportunities. These were translated into other languages within a very short time. Also, magazines were published and films were made. And as the demand was obviously continuing unabated, it was inevitable that more and more countries were to develop an interest in the airbrush market.

But of course the content was even more important than the language. As there are still very few opportunities for immediate practical training, it is the purpose of this book to serve as a substitute for a tutor and to enable the reader to study and work. I can still remember pretty accurately from my own time of learning and experimenting what I would have liked to have known and read about in order to make progress. And so I decided to write a book about just that.

C. Michael Mette

1.1 The Professional Profile of the Illustrator

I deliberately decided to discuss this question at the beginning of the book, because it is one that every budding young illustrator will have to think about right at the beginning of his career. And it is the question of training which poses the first difficult problems.

The novice is bound to have a rather hazy idea of his future job, and this is inevitable because no one has as yet succeeded in giving a comprehensive job description of what it means to be an illustrator. This applies to the whole area of graphic design. There have been a number of attempts to remedy this state of affairs, though none of them have been successful. Before giving an outline of the various types of training, I would therefore like to describe briefly what the profession of an airbrush artist actually involves.

The services of an illustrator are usually needed whenever it is impossible to take photographs. For example, it is impossible to photograph the inside of a piece of machinery or the human body. Or imagine you needed a close-up of a bat in flight with its mouth wide open and showing its fangs. A photographer's hair would probably turn grey before the right moment arrived for his picture. Also things frequently have to be depicted which do not even exist yet. Take architecture: a new congress centre can be painted a lot quicker than it can be built. And this can be done quite accurately, with plants and trees as well as people. With a picture of the end-result before one's very eyes, it is a lot easier to decide between different plans.

The last example in particular shows that illustrations can be employed for purposes other than advertising.

As well as purely commercial illustrations, this book also includes works from the spheres of art, book and magazine illustration, fashion, architecture, technology and medicine. And there are many more areas.

What are the skills that an illustrator ought to have before embarking on this career? Let me first of all do away with one particular prejudice: it is not absolutely necessary for the novice to be good at drawing before he starts training. Rather, drawing is something that can be learned during the actual training itself. What cannot be learned, however, is a feeling for form, colour and space. These are areas where you do have to be talented. And this is the talent which is tested in the dreaded entrance exams to graphic art colleges – and certainly not the ability to paint or draw.

1.2. Self-Tuition

If a person finds the prospect of entrance exams rather daunting, then it may be better for him not to train at a college. There are in fact quite a number of good illustrators who taught themselves. Some of them come from professional backgrounds that have absolutely nothing to do with illustrating. For example, I know a doctor of medicine who used to produce his own illustrations for the lectures he gave. He has since become so skilful that he is now one of the most renowned medical illustrators.

It is important for the self-taught illustrator to cover as wide a spectrum of learning as possible. Do not hesitate to take a look at a printer's or lithographer's workshop. Nowadays most of them are willing to allow students to come on work experience for a limited period of time. The more easily your work can be put into practice, the more it will be in demand one day.

Also, it is plausible and perhaps even more important to gather wide experience in the different genres. As for myself, I can say that I learnt a great deal simply by copying the old masters, though it goes without saying that the modern ones are just as useful. It is advisable to get hold of masses of material and then to work out the technique which lies behind these illustrations.

1.3 Training as a Retoucher or Producer of Composition Patterns

It is obvious that to be successful, one needs to cultivate one's skills and this need not necessarily be done in the form of self-tuition. If a person decides to train in a closely related profession, e.g. retouching or in the production of composition patterns, he should not leave his tools behind at the workshop. If you take your sketch pad with you wherever you go, you are by no means wasting your spare time but making sure that you will be able to enjoy it more fully one day. After all, success is not just a matter of talent but also of effort.

Always bear in mind that it is wrong to say you've made it just because you've come to the end of your training. In the course of your professional career – which can be anything up to 50 years – you will continually learn new things. If a person has stopped learning, he has stopped living! Also, avoid turning into someone who keeps battling on all on his own. Many well-known illustrators regret having done this, and most of them admit that it was their own fault. Try to communicate whenever possible.

Times have changed a lot since the days when everybody used to jealously guard his territory, fiercely defending it against outsiders. It is especially the "old hands" of our trade who have long since come to the conclusion that far more is to be gained than lost simply by exchanging ideas and learning from other people's experience.

1.4 Seminars and Private Colleges

Another source of training is the great variety of short seminars which are being offered more and more widely today. Airbrush seminars in particular are mushrooming all over the place. Dealers in graphic art who are more dedicated usually know which course is given where and how good it is. If I had had such an opportunity when I was beginning to work with the airbrush, I would have saved myself one or two years of experimenting with a tool I knew absolutely nothing about.

So much for the various types of training which are accessible without A levels. Nowadays there are only a small number of private colleges which are less strict in demanding A levels.

1.5 Polytechnics and Universities

Most private colleges that teach graphic design and illustration as well as all polytechnics and universities do, however, expect A levels or some equivalent thereof. It is very rare for a specially talented candidate to find his way into such an institution without these qualifications.

Understandably, the emphasis tends to be on theory. But it has been a matter of experience that it is much easier to assimilate theoretical information if a person has a certain amount of practical knowledge. This means that it is a great advantage if a university course is preceded by training in a related job.

Let me say a few words about theory. Some practical-minded people are rather contemptuous about it – wrongly! It makes a job a lot easier if you know about the things which do not lay themselves open to your immediate practical influence. Imagine, for instance, you did not know anything about human anatomy, i.e. how the different joints and muscles are built and how they work. This would mean that to draw an arm correctly you would always need to look at a picture of it, depending on movement. If, however, you knew which muscles were used for lifting a weight you could apply your knowledge and draw the arm correctly without looking at a picture.

It therefore follows that theory should be accompanied by practice and vice versa.

1.6 Duration of Training and Qualification

Originally I was going to say a few words here about the amount of time that it takes to become an illustrator. However, I find it rather difficult to generalize because each of the educational paths which I have outlined above can differ a lot. It seems that a certain course or a training period just takes three years – but is that really the end of it? A good illustrator at least will hardly ever be totally satisfied with his own work, and so he will constantly try to learn new things.

As far as the value of various training qualifications and degrees is concerned, this is something to be left to the judgement of my readers. I do not believe that it matters whether a designer has a B.A. after his name. Rather, what is far more important is the actual work he produces. Good work will be paid well, regardless of the letters after a person's name.

1.7 Some Basic Accountancy

Then there is the question of payment: most people who are creative tend to be bad or mediocre at running a business. And yet everyone is proud of having produced a good piece of work within a short time – an achievement which should be rewarded accordingly. In fact this would not have been possible without long

years of training and of gathering experience. This is something which every customer will be able to appreciate. After all, who paid for his experience with his own time? The illustrator himself, surely. Again, this is something which most customers will be able to see. Therefore you should avoid false modesty.

Make an exact calculation of the costs which are incurred while you are working on a commission. Do not forget such trivial matters as rent, even if it is not payable until the first of the next month. Or your car, even if you paid for it ages ago. Sometime in the future you will need a new car – and how are you going to finance it unless you include such costs in your calculations?

Whenever I offer a customer an estimate, I base it on a daily rate. This could be more or less, depending on the designer's qualifications. I always assume a working day of seven hours to enable me to calculate hourly rates, even though I hardly ever need them, as very few commissions can be done in a couple of hours. The greater your experience, the easier you will find it to give an estimate of the amount of time that will be necessary.

If you realize while you are working that you have made a mistake in your calculations, you should let the customer know immediately and get a statement from him that he is aware that the price will be higher. Both are best done in writing. What is important, though – and should really go without saying – is that you do not make the customer pay for your own lack of experience or your own mistakes. You may get away with it once, but the word soon gets around and it will be counterproductive in the long run.

1.8 Other Sources of Information

There is not enough space in this book to discuss this interesting topic at any great length. However, other books have been written about this, and the various professional organizations can give you further information.

1.9 Specialization – yes or no?

Finally, there is one other point I would like to discuss. This is the question of specialization. Most of the illustrators whom I know are able to tackle almost any problem that is put to them. This is because they could not afford to be choosy at the beginning of their careers.

Nevertheless, almost everyone develops certain areas after a while where he is particularly competent. With the vast amount of information that can and has to be rendered visually, it is impossible for a conscientious illustrator not to specialize. The earlier you specialize, the better. Experience shows that artists who are especially capable in a certain field tend to be handed on from one customer to another and from agency to agency, and they soon build up a reputation. However, you do not need to worry that you might have to produce the same pictures again and again. This is a profession which will always offer plenty of variety.

A collection of beautiful pictures can never be more than a picture book. What I wanted to write, however, was a picture book that one could work with. Inevitably, a large portion of it will therefore be devoted to airbrush technique.

The principles which I have worked out in the various sections are so general that there should be no problem in applying them to other tasks. There would be no point if the reader could follow the various procedures but did not know how to apply them to different situations. It is precisely this general applicability which should serve the reader as the basis for his further work with the airbrush.

2.1 Choice of Subjects

Let us start at the beginning. One of the most widespread problems – and I remember it from my own days as a novice – is that of finding suitable subjects. Especially at the beginning of your career, you are unlikely to have so many commissions that it will be no problem to you. And idleness leads to stagnation. But even when an illustrator is not faced with a concrete task, he should aim to perfect his skills. Many of the so-called "self-promotion" works have been created during such dry periods. While, as a student, you had your teacher to set you a task, now you have to do it yourself.

The first thing to do is to look for subjects. You may spend hours browsing through books and magazines, without any definite idea of what you are actually looking for, only to come to the discouraging conclusion that you have still not found that spark of an idea that you need for an illustration. This stage, however, can be simplified considerably if a more systematic approach is adopted.

Most colleagues gradually accumulate a whole archive of subjects, which are arranged and catalogued like a good library. With such a collection you can save hours of useless searching. So I would like to make a few suggestions as to how an archive can be put together.

In the first place, you need a reference framework that will give you an idea of the various subject areas at one glance. You can have headings such as "People", "Animals", "Landscape", "Technology", etc. The next step is to sub-divide these areas and to create lower levels of classification. "People", for example, can be sub-divided into "Women", "Men", "Children", or alternatively into "Old People" and "Young People" or into "Europeans", "Africans", "Chinese", etc. You should, however, decide beforehand how you want to divide each area.

On the third level you may want to divide the subject area "Men" into "Old Men" and "Young Men" and then into "Europeans" and "Africans", or first into groups of race and then age. If, however, you do not start your classification until you are actually looking for subjects, you are likely to get confused. Dividing and sub-dividing a given subject area in this way is known as a tree diagram. It is the same principle which is used by computers – and it is by no means inpossible that a time will come when your archive is so large that you want to use a computer to find your subjects. In fact, you may want to bear this in mind from the very onset.

Do not be frustrated if, at the beginning of your classification, you keep thinking of new ideas of how you might proceed. This is quite normal. Allow yourself several options before committing yourself to one particular structure of your collection. Make a diagram like the one below. You may even find that you can use your airbrush for a diagram that shows the various levels. I have in fact seen a number of good examples of how this can be done in a book called "DIAGRAMS".

The next step is of a very practical kind: where are you going to put your collection of subjects? I would suggest that you start a number of files. This has the advan-

SUBJECTS

ANIMATE BEINGS   THINGS

ANIMALS PEOPLE PLANTS

MEN WOMAN CHILDREN

WHOLE BODIES   PARTS OF THE BODY

FACE HANDS FEET

EYES MOUTH HAIR

Ill. 1

tage that you can extend and re-arrange your collection again and again. Also, it forces you to limit yourself to a manageable format.

When you have prepared everything, you can start searching and collecting. And next time you are looking for a particular subject – say, for a certain job you have been commissioned to do – you should have one of your classificatory headings in mind. Either cut out the pictures you have found or note down where you found which picture on which topic. Always proceed in small steps. Never look for more than one particular kind of subject, or you will get confused. Your collection will soon get larger. I remember that my own collection reached about a thousand pictures within my first year alone.

If you work consistently, you will not only build up an extensive collection but you will also practice your ability to persevere. Perseverance is one of the most important qualities that are needed to become a really good illustrator. It is only with a good deal of stubbornness and persistence that you get to a stage where you are not thrown off balance by the slightest little thing.

Whenever I had to choose subjects for a free illustration, I used to make the same mistake again and again, i.e. I attempted too much. There is of course nothing wrong in wanting to draw from as many resources as possible, but the more complex the subject, the greater the number of difficulties which are involved.

At the beginning of a certain job one can still overcome many obstacles by means of one's enthusiasm, but as the work goes on the various sources of errors might increase and can easily slow down one's progress quite considerably. It is a great pity if you put a lot of effort into a job and then cannot achieve your own objectives in the end.

Therefore I suggest that you choose simple topics as long as you are not totally confident. If you are consistently successful in small matters, this will have a cumulative effect and provide the sort of incentive that will gradually make you a good illustrator.

2.2 Preparing a Sketch

Once you have decided on a particular subject, you should start with a few small, swiftly-drawn sketches. Forget about the airbrush for the time being. Simply produce some conventional sketches with a pencil or a crayon. Make sure you plan the structure of your drawing. You need not work from one single, coherent picture to make your sketch, you may prefer to use details from several pictures and then put them together.

However, there is one thing you ought to avoid: never try to draw everything from memory. There are of course certain subjects which you have at your fingertips, simply because you have drawn them so many times, but that is a matter of experience. Even the great masters of our profession do not hesitate to copy. Do feel free to use technical aids such as an epidiascope or various re-drawing devices. This will leave you free to concentrate on the problems inherent in the airbrush technique. Later, when you have acquired enough experience, you can begin to impress others with drawings from memory.

In particular, your sketches should show the distribution of light and dark and shadows. To start with, you may want to dissolve a subject into its contrasting areas. In fact, you should pay less attention to their forms than to their tone values. Later, you will find that the order in which you proceed in masking is directly dependent upon the distribution of tone values.

At this stage you need not pay any great attention to working out all the details. Just relax and start drawing in an unhurried, leisurely way. The finer points will follow eventually anyway. To be as relaxed as possible, you should practice a lot with your pencil or felt pen. Practice drawing different kinds of hatchings and bold curves. These need not be planned intellectually, but should be a matter of your feelings, your "guts", so to speak. When you draw long lines, you should follow a

simple rule: the joint which you move should be as far away from the paper as possible, because the further away it is, the broader and more regular your lines will be.

You can easily try this out. Stand in front of your drawing table and try to use only your shoulder joint when you are drawing a line. Then draw the same line moving your wrist. The difference will be quite considerable.

When your first sketches are satisfactory you can go one step further and compose a general picture from the best of your studies. This can be rather more elaborated, and a number of general points are worth noting.

2.3 Planning and Making a Mask

The airbrush technique has one particular feature which most novices tend to find a downright nuisance. It is the simple fact that you cannot really judge the success of your work until the last layer has been applied to the final mask. Until then you can only have a very vague idea of the eventual outcome.

Many colleagues, including some of the more famous ones, have found a way round this disadvantage by introducing a number of intermediary stages. In doing so they "un-mask", as it were, their works so that they take a good look at it and plan the further steps. They are perfectly aware that this takes away from the speed which characterizes the airbrush technique and which is one of its most obvious assets. After all, they have to stick it all together again and cut new masks before they can continue working. Nevertheless, this procedure is of great benefit to the final result.

The number of intermediary steps can be reduced considerably if the sketches are worked out in as much detail as possible. What is particularly important here is the distribution of tone values at the edges where two totally separate areas meet. Depending on the colours, it will often be possible to restrict oneself to one or two masks for several areas that are similar in tone. I shall illustrate this with an example.

2.4 An Example of a Mask

Let us assume an illustration (ill. 2) consists of four areas which are different in value but have similar shades. One way in which these areas can be airbrushed will be immediately plausible. You simply cover all areas with masking film, except for the one you are going to work on, and spray on your paint. Next, you remove the mask and put a new one on, again leaving open just one area, and then you spray on your second colour. Finally, you do the same with the third and the fourth area.

But there is in fact an easier way. Take any of the three areas and compare it with the neighbouring ones. If you find an adjacent area where the edge that borders on the first one is darker, then continue your comparison in the same way, using the second area as the basis. In our example you should find eventually that it does not border on any darker area. This is the area you should now call number one, or rather "Step One" or "Stage One".

You should now disregard this area and compare the remaining ones, using the method described above. The result should be a scale ranging from one to four. And this is the order in which the areas can then be sprayed.

You start off by unmasking and spraying the area you have now called number one, and then, without having to cover up the first one again, you do the same with two, three and four. This does indeed work without

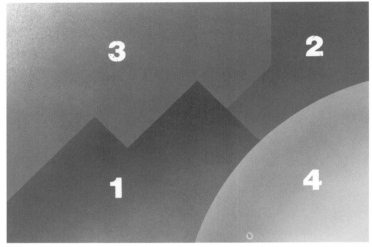

Ill. 2

having to cover the areas that have been sprayed already. Just try it out. The four areas in our example have been numbered already so that it can be checked.

The more accurate and detailed your study sketches are, the less you have to insert intermediary stages to find out how the illustration is developing. This is because your sketches have given you a fair idea already.

So far as the sketches are concerned, I have only mentioned the distribution of light and darkness in them. To determine the order of the masking stages, a simple black-and-white drawing will normally be sufficient. However, you may find it helpful for planning the masks to elaborate your sketches a little further, using colour, though this depends on the colours you want to use in the picture. This will have to be discussed further at a later stage.

2.5 Making a Mask Drawing

The next important step is to make one or more mask drawings. I am talking here about the kind of masks that are to be cut with self-adhesive masking film later on. If the sketches are adequate, this should not be much of a problem.

If the masking material firmly covers the ground while you are spraying the rest of an area, then the edge will quite automatically be a sharp one. Or at least most of the time. Sometimes there is a very slight fuzziness. This tends to happen because not all the sprayed paint sticks to the surface, instead a few particles are blown about by the air pressure in the airbrush and then settle on the entire unmasked area.

Self-adhesive masks are only suitable for areas which are separated from their neighbouring areas by a sharp edge. These dividing lines between two areas which differ in tone value should become obvious from the sketches. It is along these lines that the masks are cut. If you want a softer transition, there are different techniques which will be discussed later.

Put a piece of tracing paper on your sketch and then trace the dividing lines with a fairly soft, but very sharp pencil. In the first stage you do this for all the areas, regardless of the colours that will fill them eventually. The sketch that you have now produced is your basic mask. To make sure that this mask and the subsequent ones are always exactly in place, it is advisable to put in a few marks at this stage. These can be transferred onto the other masks.

2.6 Planning Your Colours and Making a Masking Script

From a purely theoretical point of view, it should be possible to make do with no more than four masks, just as in printing, i.e. one each for the three prime colours yellow, magenta and cyan, as well as another one for black, to add darkness. But this would only make life unnecessarily hard. After all, there is usually a fairly large range of colours at your disposal so that you do

not have to mix every single nuance. Nor would it be particularly efficient, on the other hand, if you were to cut a separate mask for each colour that occurs. As with everything, you have to find the happy medium and it is one of the marks of a good illustrator if he has achieved this. On the whole, it is largely a question of experience.

Once you have drawn your basic mask, you have to do some brainwork again. Try to get a very clear idea as to which areas are similar in colour shade. These can usually be sprayed in a single stage, using only one mask. They can gradually be unmasked, using the scheme described above, and then worked on. The reason why they have to be similar in colour shade is because the areas that have already been sprayed are not going to be covered up again and they will therefore have tiny amounts of paint sprayed onto them. In fact it is advisable to write down the order of the various stages, perhaps on a copy of the mask drawing.

This written plan is what I call my "airbrush script", and once it is fixed, I stick to it. Experience shows that one tends to make fewer mistakes at the planning or stage, brainwork than on the actual job itself. You have probably noticed that I wrote "fewer mistakes": obviously there can never be a guarantee that errors will be eliminated altogether.

Most works will include several areas which are similar in their colour shades, e.g. one in red, another in blue, and perhaps a third one in green. If this is the case, you will have to make a mask for each area. Use the sketch on your basic mask and do not forget the markings. Again, make your drawings on tracing paper with a soft, well-sharpened pencil.

There is of course no reason why you should not include colour in your sketches. Many colours can be mixed by spraying a small number of basic colours on top of each other. This technique is known as glazing. What is important is that the individual colours should be transparent, such as glaze, or they should be made transparent. This can be done by thinning them down so much that they no longer cover a surface in one single layer. The particles of the pigment have to be so far apart from one another that the surface will shine through them.

Now imagine that your illustration contains one blue and one yellow area, both of them similar in shade, as well as several different shades of green. In order to achieve clean, unadulterated shades of blue and yellow you need at least two masks. It should be possible to include the various green shades in these two masking stages. And this can be simulated beforehand by simply using coloured pencils. All you have to do is draw hatchings of different density on a white surface and allow some of these hatchings to overlap.

The shade which you finally airbrush onto your illustration should be identical with the one on your sketch, if at all possible. To compare the one with the other, you should hold your sketch against the sprayed area at short intervals. Thus, in the above example, you can do without a third mask for those areas of green that are similar in shade. However, before applying this principle to a more complex job, you should practise it in an exercise that involves simple colour areas. The time you spend practising will not have been wasted.

To conclude: You start off with a very simple subject. Gradually, by means of several sketches, you feel your way towards a composition of your picture. Once you have a final sketch, you must make your mask drawing and plan your various masking stages. Not until you have done all this can you start working on the actual picture itself.

2.7 Preliminaries

First of all, make sure you can clean your work surface with methylated spirits. If you now transferred your mask drawing straight onto the board by means of carbon paper, you would probably have a hard job getting rid of the black lines again later on. There is a simpler or more efficient way of transferring a mask drawing.

Cut out a sheet of masking film so that it is large enough to cover the entire illustration. Then take off the protective paper and put the film on the work surface with the adhesive side facing upwards. Stick on the mask drawing, facing downwards, and press the pencil lines firmly into the adhesive layer with a bone folder.

When you separate the two sheets again, you will find that there is a faint residue of carbon on the adhesive surface of the masking film. Having thus prepared your film you can now mask the entire board which you are about to work with. You should find that the mask drawing is sufficiently visible. Also, you cannot wipe it off by mistake when you are cutting the various masks.

In the next chapter you will learn about a further method of transferring a mask drawing.

The next step: cutting. What I am going to tell you now will sound rather simple, although it is in fact pretty difficult. Make sure you do not damage the board while you are cutting! If there are any dents or grooves in the board, the paint will collect in them and you will have some rather ugly contours.

To practice this technique I used to use up vast quantities of balloons. These are really ideal. Simply stick a piece of masking film onto an inflated balloon and try cutting it without bursting the balloon – this really is the best way of practising.

Always cut all the lines of a mask before applying the first layer of paint. If you have left out a line you might easily spray over it and then have difficulties finding it again. With a good scalpel the line which you cut should be fine enough not to allow paint to penetrate to the board.

2.8 Spraying Your Picture

Once you have fixed the order of the various stages in advance, I would urge you to keep to this order. This may be rather difficult at first, but you will probably soon find that such a procedure simplifies the whole job tremendously. And when you have been successful several times, you will undoubtedly feel a lot more self-confident.

When we went to school, most of us were taught to start a picture in the top left-hand corner and finish it in the lower right-hand corner. As a good airbrush artist, you should get rid of this idea as quickly as possible.

To be able to compare the various elements of a picture and to balance them against one another, it is necessary to work in different layers. And that applies to the entire illustration. The order of the individual stages is determined by your masking script. There is no point in trying to finish off each element before proceeding to the next one. Simply work out as much as necessary to determine the form and the colour. The details should be left until the very end.

Copying pictures will teach you quite a lot about this technique. This does not mean that you have to stick slavishly to the original in order to gather experience. There are many paths that lead to Rome, and if you think you have found a better one, you should use it.

2.9 Preserving and Protecting Your Pictures

The final question in this chapter is that of protecting an airbrush picture. If the paint has been applied relatively lightly, the surface may easily suffer. Even finger-prints can have rather disastrous consequences.

The majority of airbrush illustrations are made for the purpose of reproduction and therefore only need to be preserved for a limited length of time. As soon as the slides or lithographs have been made, the originals can be stored flat in a dark drawer – unless they have already become ugly to look at. With pictures like this it is advisable to cover them with a thin plastic foil or a layer of protective varnish.

It is a different matter if a picture is to be hung up on a wall and is likely to get exposed to a harmful environment for a longer time. If this is the case, the picture should be mounted and put under protective UV glass. If the paint is likely to fade, a layer of protective UV varnish should be sprayed on. These things are available in special shops.

The best protection, however, is to choose an extremely light-proof paint that becomes insoluble as soon as it is dry. And yet, after a while, even these pictures have to be specially protected in a darkened room where they are put behind glass and kept from people who might be rather too curious. The Mona Lisa is a good example. If Leonardo had been able to use an airbrush at the time, he would probably have done so.

3.1 "The Peach" by Norbert Cames

So far I have only given you verbal information about how an airbrush picture is created. This will now be illustrated by an example. We shall take a look at the complete process of one particular airbrush picture, with comments by Norbert Cames, the artist.

Although every illustrator gradually acquires his own style in the course of his career, it is nevertheless true to say that, on the whole, most illustrators follow a fairly similar procedure. "The Peach" can therefore be taken as reasonably representative, and this is what Norbert Cames says about it:

"When I chose the paint for this illustration, I decided to use a very opaque one. It had to be water-resistant when it was dry, and light-proof. And so it seemed sensible to use acrylics.

As a ground I chose some extra thick illustration line board, which is particularly suitable for scraping and does not become uneven very quickly.

To transfer the sketch, I made my own tracing paper in the colour that was most useful. With a piece of cotton wool I rubbed some fine pigment from coloured pencils onto the tracing paper. This meant that I did not need to erase these lines later on."

The various stages have been numbered and are accompanied by an explanatory text.

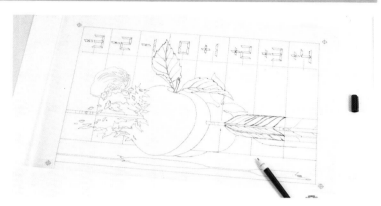

3.2 Stages in the Procedure

1. The colour layout need not be absolutely impeccable. The object is merely to get an idea of the general impression and to be able to plan the individual stages.

2. The mask drawing is then made with the help of the colour sketch. To avoid blurring the lines, it is advisable to use a water-colour pen. Later, these will be traced onto the illustration ground.

3. In a number of individual steps, the sketch is then gradually transferred onto the board. To make sure everything is exactly in position, I put crosses onto the board and the tracing paper with a sheet of carbon paper. These will have to be protected throughout the entire procedure with some adhesive transparent tape.

4. Using the home-made tracing paper in the appropriate colour (see above), the drawing is then transferred step by step and covered with self-adhesive masking film. Whenever a portion of the illustration is to be worked on, it is cut out with a scalpel, unmasked and then sprayed.

5. At this stage it is still too early to work out the finer details. The exact colours and technical nuances will be tackled later.

6. When the first layer of protective film has been removed, the individual details are refined further, but they are not given their final form.

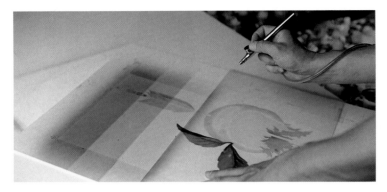

7. The subject itself is now 70 % finished and is covered with protective masking film. Also, the edges of the format are now fixed with self-adhesive tape.

8. The ground is covered with stable, non-adhesive, transparent masking film and sprayed step by step, beginning with the darkest parts and then gradually proceeding to the light ones.

9. At last the overall effect – especially of the colour – can be assessed more easily, and the details can be worked out more accurately. The structure of the feather with its brown line on the yellow background is now to be elaborated.

10. Except for the red parts of the feather, the illustration is masked again. Areas of paint are applied with the airbrush, and the general structure is reinforced with a paint-brush.

11. To get an idea of the overall impression, the illustration is now stripped completely of all its masking film and stencils.

12. It has become obvious that the background of the peach is too light and has to be reinforced with more yellow. Then the resultant glare is carefully erased.

13. The fine, vein-like red skin of the peach can be sprayed very nicely with a fine airbrush. Those parts which are particularly delicate can be done extremely effectively with a coloured pencil or some crayon.

14. In the next step, white paint is airbrushed onto those areas which are meant to be lighter than others.

15. The final adjustments can begin, and the general effect has become quite easy to judge. With a paint-brush, a number of individual details can be readjusted so that they fit in better. It is at this stage that one can see the advantage of choosing fast-drying, water-resistant colours.

16. To spray the soft contours of the shadow, the stencil has to be held above the illustration board at some small distance. This distance can be achieved very efficiently with the help of paper tissues placed underneath the stencil. However, the pressure of the airbrush might shift the stencil, so it has to be weighted down with metal strips.

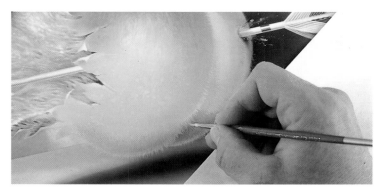

17. To add the final touch, the paintbrush is used again. Here you can see the tiny hairs of the peach being painted on.

18. The sharp contours of the numbers are done right at the end. Before they can be airbrushed, the whole picture has to be masked again. Then the contours can be drawn onto the film with ordinary carbon paper and the numbers can be cut out. To get a better idea of which colour should be used, a piece of paper with a sample is held against the area.

4.1 A Brief Outline

I f we wanted to list every single airbrush that is used in the world, we would have enough material for another book. I shall therefore limit myself to the ones that are used by the illustrators mentioned here. Neither will I list all the technical data, but only the names, types, manufacturers, the width of the nozzles and the size of the reservoirs. And I would like to em-phasize right at the beginning that the quality of the work does not depend on that of the airbrush being used.

Depending on the task, a particular airbrush will be more or less suitable. For instance, it would be rather foolhardy to work on a very large area with a 0.1 mm nozzle, and it would be equally difficult to tackle delicate nuances with a 0.8 mm nozzle. This is why most artists who regularly use the airbrush always have several.

Name	Type	Manufacturer	Width of nozzle	Size of reservoir
Conopois	F	Conopois Instruments Ltd, Worthington,	0.15 mm	2 cm^3
Aerograph	63A	DeVilbiss, Bournemouth, Hampshire, U.K.	0.15 mm	1 cm^3
	63E		0.25 mm	5 cm^3
Sprite	Junior		0.25 mm	3 cm^3
	Major		0.30 mm	7 cm^3
EFBE	Type A	Friedrich Boldt, Hanover, West Germany	0.15 mm	1 cm^3
	Type B1		0.30 mm	6 cm^3
	Type C1		0.30 mm	6 cm^3
Fischer	Set GI83	Fischer by LETRASET, Paris, France	0.20 mm	3 cm^3
			0.30 mm	15 cm^3
			0.40 mm	60 cm^3
Grafo	11B	Grafo-Feinmechanik, Kronberg, West Germany	0.30 mm	6 cm^3
IWATA	HP-A	IWATA, Tokyo, Japan	0.20 mm	1 cm^3
	HP-B		0.20 mm	2 cm^3
	HP-C		0.30 mm	7 cm^3
	HP-BE1		0.60 mm	40 cm^3
OLYMPOS	100 B	OLYMPOS Co. Ltd.,	0.20 mm	2 cm^3
	SP-B		0.30 mm	7 cm^3
Paasche	V1	Paasche Airbrush Co.,	0.25 mm	1 cm^3
	VL-1		0.25 mm	7 cm^3
	Turbo			
Thayer &	A	Thayer & Chandler, Chicago, U.S.A.	0.20 mm	4 cm^3
Ultra	F15	Harder & Steinbeck, Hamburg, West Germany	0.30 mm	10 cm^3

The medium which we use is the rapidly flowing air which passes from the compressor through a hose into the airbrush. It runs below the pigment reservoir as far as the nozzle. Shortly before the nozzle the passage is slightly larger so that the air can flow evenly around the entire nozzle.

The amount of air is regulated by means of a highly sensitive valve on the connecting piece between the airbrush and the hose. The valve can be opened by pressing the jet switch downwards. The counter-pressure is provided by a small spring. This allows you to work in a variety of different ways. The stronger the air pressure at the nozzle, the finer will be the atomized pigment when it is sucked out of the reservoir. Conversely, when only a small amount of pressure is applied, the paint drops will be correspondingly larger.

4.2 How an Airbrush is Made and How it Works

How does it actually work? Although the technology of it is rather complicated, it is in fact quite a simple gadget. The physical laws that are involved were described for the first time by a Swiss physicist called Daniel Bernouilli. Therefore it is also known as the Bernouilli effect. To express it in as simple terms as possible: if a medium is fast flowing, negative pressure will be created around it. The following sectional drawing will make it easier for you to understand this.

At this point I would like to mention one particular mistake which is frequently made. The amount of paint which is sprayed on the surface does not depend on the degree of air pressure. The pressure really only de-

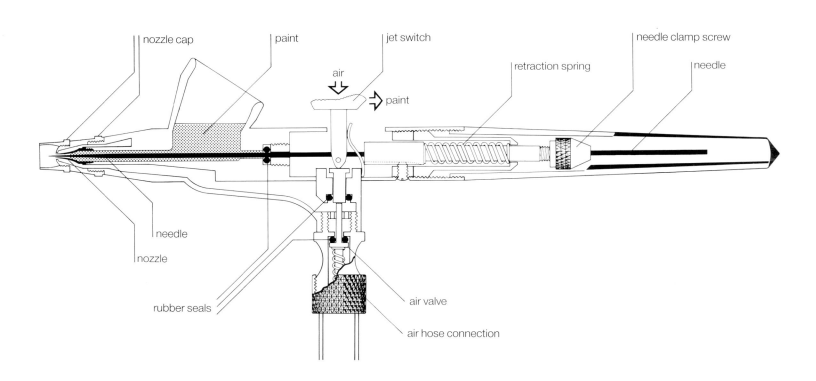

termines how fine the atomized particles are going to be.

The amount of paint that flows is controlled separately. Inside the entire airbrush there is a movable needle. The front end of this needle is sharpened conically. It is linked to the jet switch by means of a small piston and a clamp screw. If you pull the switch with your finger, the needle moves in the same direction. A spring then automatically pulls it back into the same position.

A close look at the diagram reveals that the opening of the nozzle gets narrower and narrower towards the front. This means that when the needle is as far to the front as it will go, the aperture will be hermetically closed. When the needle is pulled back, an open space is created between it and the nozzle wall which expands even further when the needle is pulled further back. It is this space, and nothing else, that determines how much paint is going to be sprayed.

So remember: pressing the jet switch downwards increases the air pressure and results in finer atomization. Pulling it forward or backward increases the nozzle aperture and thus the amount of paint. Both functions are independent of each other.

Beside the double-action switch described above there is also a single-action one, where retraction simultaneously opens the valve by means of an eccentric. The principle here is: the more paint, the more air. This type of airbrush is gradually becoming obsolete, but is still being manufactured. Depending on which airbrush you used as a student, you will find that it takes some time to get used to a different one. This probably explains why so many old hands among the illustrators virtually swear by "their" own particular type of airbrush.

For the sake of completeness, I shall have to mention one airbrush that does not make use of the Bernouilli effect. This is the Paasche Turbo, which is also called the Rolls Royce among the airbrushes. Instead of following the suction principle, the paint is carried by a rapidly moving transport needle straight to the nozzle, which is indeed merely an air nozzle, and then sprayed onto the illustration ground.

We do not need to describe this type of airbrush any further because it is too complicated and too rare. Suffice it here to point out its assets. Given that you have had plenty of practice, you can draw lines and dots with it which are no wider than a tenth of a millimetre. It would be dangerous, though, to jump to the conclusion that a finer airbrush automatically yields better results. Like any other tool, perhaps even more so, it requires a great deal of expertise. Otherwise it would be like buying a racing car to take a letter to the post office round the corner.

4.3 Possible Errors – and How to Avoid Them

Although the airbrush is not particularly difficult to use, there are nevertheless quite a number of mistakes that one can make. Unfortunately, such errors are bound to occur whenever a considerable amount of time has been invested in an illustration. Two or three delicately placed highlights after a week of hard work – and some stupid instrument "spits" at them and ruins everything.

It is worth noting at this point that over eighty percent of all errors are caused by insufficient cleaning and maintenance of the instrument. Paint which has been made liquid and sprayable by means of some bonding agent or thinner does happen to have the unfortunate tendency to dry in the open air. And also inside the airbrush itself. It clogs and settles inside the nozzle and onto the needle. After a while, the various apertures become smaller and smaller until they are blocked up completely.

Depending on the paint, the only thing that might help in such a case is probably ultrasound treatment. Avoid cleaning the airbrush with extremely acid material or with a knife, a steel brush or a sand-blast unit. It is too sensitive an instrument to survive such treatment unscathed.

A simple clog is still relatively harmless, for although the airbrush refuses to ejaculate paint, at least there are no disasters. What is far worse is a case where a loose lump of pigment or dirt blocks up the inside of the nozzle and then detaches itself at precisely that moment when you have desperately retracted the needle to make the airbrush work again. The same thing can aslo happen when the pressure is increased.

4.4 How to Clean the Airbrush

The best and simplest way of avoiding these pitfalls is to clean your airbrush regularly. Never allow the paint to dry inside the instrument. Instead, you should clean it with the solvent that is appropriate to each kind of pigment, using cotton buds. Thus a few seconds can in fact save you hours of unnecessary work.

The critical points of an airbrush are its narrowest passages and those areas which are most exposed to air. The paint always dries particularly quickly at the tip of the needle, which is continually surrounded by air. It should be wiped clean with your thumb and index finger every five minutes. The nozzle, tube and reservoir should be cleaned thoroughly at least every thirty minutes.

Also make sure that no paint reaches the air valve or the switch mechanism. Always put the airbrush down in such a way that the nozzle is slightly below the switch, and avoid extremely sudden movements so that the paint does not suddenly squirt out of the reservoir. Thus you can also protect your clothes.

Another common malfunction is often caused by a mechanical defect of the needle, especially the tip. Unless it is absolutely straight, it will disturb the mixture of paint and air that flows past it so much that it becomes impossible to have any control over your work. The tip of the needle can easily be bent if it is re-inserted carelessly after cleaning. But I do not think it is necessary to explain how this can be avoided.

A bent needle can be temporarily restored with the help of a bone folder, but it will never be as good as new again. Needles, like nozzles, are subject to wear and tear. Always have two or three new needles ready, as well as at least one nozzle. Once you feel you are spending too much money on these accessories, you will no doubt be more careful with your equipment.

Incidentally, there are two types of nozzles: one with a screw fitting and one self-centring. The former is screwed on with a small spanner, while the latter is held in place by the nozzle cap which, in turn, is screwed onto the airbrush.

Both types of constructions have their enthusiasts. It is said that the self-centring nozzle always screws on in such a way that the needle is exactly in the middle, which means that the airbrushed result will be of superior quality. Also, the needle can be inserted from the front so that it is less likely to get damaged. Screw-fitted nozzles, on the other hand, do not need additional rubber seals which might get lost easily or become brittle. Not wanting to give a value judgement myself, I would say that the differences are not really discernible with the naked eye.

One particularly useful little accessory deserves to be mentioned at this point, the airbrush holder. Nearly every airbrush manufacturer offers it in one form or another. When you buy one, make sure that it is fully adjustable so that it can be fixed anywhere. It should be possible to fix it to the edge of a table or a chair with a clamp or a stop screw. Important: the airbrush should always be held by the holder in such a way that it is slightly below the jet switch. This is the only way of preventing paint from running down the needle channel and into the air valve.

There is not enough space in this book to give more than a rather general description of airbrush technology. And the same limitation also applies to the compressor, which we shall look at now.

4.5 Compressors

In recent years the piston-operated compressor has become more and more popular. It pumps air into a storage cylinder until a certain pressure is reached. Then the machine switches itself off automatically. A pressure-reducing device ensures that the airbrush receives the amount of pressure which is necessary, depending on the type of paint that is being used.

Apart from piston-driven compressors, there are also some that employ a diaphragm principle and there are turbine compressors, all of which use storage cylinders. The latter are really only suitable for large studios and are correspondingly expensive. Diaphragm compressors, on the other hand, are being used less and less.

When buying a compressor you should examine critically whether it meets the following four requirements:

1. Does it include a moisture extraction element? This is the only way in which the rather unpleasant phenomenon of condensation can be avoided. A single little drop can ruin hours of hard work.

2. Is its capacity sufficient? How much air are you likely to need? For smaller pictures no larger than A4, for instance, you will not need more than about 0.7 cubic feet of air per minute. If, however, you want to airbrush a whole car, you will need as much as 9 to 12 cubic feet. It is advisable to choose a compressor with a capacity of about 25 percent above the amount needed.

3. How noisy is the machine? You should have it demonstrated to you before buying it. Sound-absorption technology has progressed so far these days that you can only hear a compressor when you are standing right next to it. It is of course possible to have a sound-absorber attached afterwards, but if you do so, you must make sure that there is enough flow of air!

4. Is the machine sufficiently vibration-proof? If your compressor starts walking around the studio, you can be sure that the hose will eventually become too short. This can be avoided simply by putting a rubber mat underneath the compressor.

There are not many points that have to be borne in mind when using a compressor. In order to find the most suitable degree of pressure all you have to do is keep increasing it until the result cannot be sprayed any more finely, then tighten the pressure gauge very carefully and stop as soon as the paint is getting coarser again. Add another 0.1 bars.

4.6 Cleaning and Maintenance

It is important that you should check your compressor regularly, and this includes the oil level. Normally, this should not present problems, but it may happen that the oil level keeps going down rather too fast. If this is the case, you should have the compressor serviced. Also, make sure you only use the oil which is provided by the manufacturer. Always keep to the instructions, or you might lose your guarantee.

Also, you should regularly take out the moisture which tends to collect in the cylinder. Sooner or later it might actually run over and, despite the moisture extraction element, penetrate into the hose. Quite apart from that, it could in fact lead to rust.

4.7 Accessories

Many manufacturers now offer compressors that can have several airbrushes attached to them. It is possible to fix self-locking quick-release couplings to the upper end of the hose. Assuming that your airbrushes have the necessary adaptors, you can then use a single hose.

4.8 Other Air-Supply Systems

Some illustrators use "tinned air" instead of compressors. These are large steel cylinders with compressed air or carbon dioxide. Depending on the size, they can last for quite some time and provide a clean, regular flow of air. When compressors were still very noisy, I used to work with such a cylinder myself. At the beginning 20 lbs. were sufficient for about four to five weeks.

The cylinder itself can be bought or rented, but in order to control the pressure it is vital to attach a pressure gauge. However, these are often so expensive that it is often cheaper to buy a compressor.

If you are not sure at this stage whether you are going to maintain your interest in the airbrush technique for any length of time, you may prefer to experiment with small propellant gas devices of the 'throwaway' type. The air in these cylinders is so highly compressed that they yield about twenty minutes. In the long run they are of course very uneconomical.

4.9 Extracting the Colour Dust

Finally , I would like to point out that there are extraction devices for the residual spray that usually settles in the studio. Depending on the paint which is used, one may in fact find such a device indispensable. There are various kinds of different sizes on the market, ranging from a table model to a whole cabin-like construction which can be used for spraying cars.

For small-format airbrush work and for using material that is common in graphic design, you will find that a dust shield is sufficient as protection, and this can be bought in any specialist shop.

In the next chapter we shall discuss the type of paint and other materials than can be used.

5.1 The Ground

Now that you are familiar with the technology of the airbrush as well as its maintenance, let us turn to all the other materials that are necessary. We shall first examine the ground, or support, for your airbrush work.

The most widely used kinds of ground are probably paper and hard board, and there are a number of criteria that should be considered for buying the most suitable kind.

First of all, there is the question of firmness. For using self-adhesive masking film the surface has to be so firm that it does not get damaged when the film is removed. Otherwise you might suddenly end up with parts of

your illustration sticking to the masking film instead of the board.

Another important point is that of absorbency. Some paints are extremely thin, such as protein-based paint and ink, and if the paper is too absorbent they just sink in and cannot achieve their full intensity. Also, it can happen that the painted areas get fuzzy edges, despite the use of masking film. Or the paint continues to flow along the cut edges like a subterranean channel and forms some ugly lines.

There are of course more than two grounds that can be used for airbrushed artwork. Illustrators often use canvas or wood. Although they can be used untreated, it is advisable to prime them first. This will ensure better and more saturated colours.

It is possible to emphasize the structure of the ground by the way in which the paint is sprayed on, i.e. by

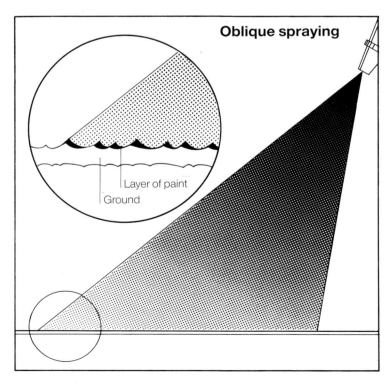

Oblique spraying

Layer of paint
Ground

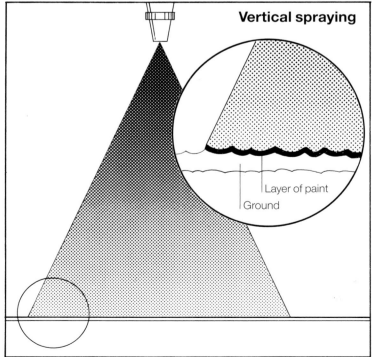

Vertical spraying

Layer of paint
Ground

30

holding the airbrush at a very acute angle. The illustration above shows the difference between pigment sprayed on vertically and at an acute angle.

Furthermore, illustrators sometimes prefer plastic or glass to canvas or hard board. As these are totally non-absorbent, it is impossible for the paint to dry away into the ground. This means that it has to be applied extremely thinly and each layer must be given time to dry before the next one can be sprayed on. Otherwise there will be an uneven surface.

Finally, it should be pointed out that, in principle, any ground will do, even cars, surf boards and china, all of which are often used by artists.

5.2 The Masking Film

The airbrush technique has had its greatest boost within the last few years, and this is undoubtedly due to the increasingly excellent quality of adhesive masking film which is now available on the market. In fact, the life of an airbrush artist has become a lot easier since the days when we were still struggling with adhesive crêpe paper and rubber cement – and that was really only a few years ago.

There are now so many different types of masking film available that it can be rather difficult to choose. However, there are a few simple criteria that will help you find the right kind of film to suit your specific purposes.

As a rule, the adhesive strength of a film should be as small as possible. Not too small, however, because otherwise the draught of air coming from the airbrush nozzle might lift it off the ground. Nevertheless, it ought to be reasonably small so that when you mask a picture several times, no colour particles get peeled off along with the film. You should ask to test your film very briefly before buying it.

There may also be the problem that when one film is stuck onto another they can only be separated again with great difficulty. This increase in adhesiveness can also occur when a film has to stay on the ground for a longer time. Should that happen, you should change to a different brand. Nowadays you can buy film which is of such a high quality that these difficulties hardly need to occur at all.

Another important point to consider is the thickness of the film. The thinner the film, the flatter will be the edges of the masked areas. On the other hand, one can easily see that the converse is also true: if the film is too strong, some of the edges might end up rather too thick. This is unlikely to have a positive effect on the overall impression of an illustration and occasionally it makes the lithographic process more difficult.

There are two types of masking film on the market: glossy and mat. If it is only used for covering areas, then the glossy variety is perfectly adequate, but I have found that if I want to draw and spray on it, then mat is more suitable.

Finally, there are also different types of material. Your film should be flexible enough to fit round uneven parts of the surface. If it is too flexible, though, there is the danger that you might damage the ground: normally one would scrape the film gently with a scalpel and then break it off, but if it is too flexible, you might only be able to cut through it.

It goes without saying that, depending on the purpose, there may be other criteria that could be important, though in most cases it is sufficient to check adhesiveness, thickness, surface and flexibility.

5.3 Stencils

Another technique which has become considerably easier over the years is the use of stencils. Stencil masks, unlike the cover-up type, generally involve non-adhesive material. Thanks to the chemical industry there has been a great deal of improvement here. Stencil work has become almost ideal with the availability of crystal-clear film that covers a wide range of different degrees of strength.

It is obviously a great advantage to be able to use stencils that are totally transparent. You can actually see what has been covered and compare it with the colour that you are spraying on at the time. There are different ways of using stencils, depending on their thickness. A 0.5 mm stencil, for instance, allows you to raise it off the surface slightly so that a softer edge can be obtained.

However, there is more to stencils than Astralon and Ultraphane. You can in fact use any three-dimensional object, and there is enormous scope for experiment.

Let me make some suggestions. The contours of cloud formations can be achieved by experimenting with the torn edge of a piece of paper. Or you could use a thick piece of cotton wool. To prevent it from blowing about in the airbrush breeze, stiffen it with some sprayed lacquer.

Cloth stencil can be useful, too. One can very easily design backgrounds by using pieces of net curtain with different patterns. People are often amazed and full of admiration at the perseverance of an illustrator working out the most minute details. You will soon find that it is worthwhile leaving the beaten track and giving free rein to your imagination in choosing your stencils.

5.4 Cutting Tools

Masking film and stencils obviously have to be cut, and for this purpose most illustrators prefer surgical scalpels. These are extremely sharp, and the cutting edges are available in many different shapes. New blades are not extraordinarily expensive and can be changed quickly. There are round, oval and flat handles.

The best cut can be achieved if you constantly apply the same pressure on a blade that is always sharp. This requires a lot of practice, and it means that the blade has to be changed relatively frequently. However, there is no other way of avoiding damage to the ground.

Most lines are cut freehand, but if you have to cut a straight line, there is no reason why you should not use a ruler. Make sure that it is a metal ruler because it will last longer. For regular curves use an ordinary ellipse guide, cutting along it very carefully.

Circles are the only shapes that really need a special tool, i.e. a compass cutter. If you are planning to buy one, make sure you do not go for mere cheapness. As you cannot put a separate blade in for every kind of radius, it has to be very sharp indeed. This means that the blade often tends to bend away to the outside and you suddenly find that the radius of your circle has grown by a few millimetres once you have gone round 360 degrees. To prevent this from happening, the joint should be very robust, which tends to make the compass cutter rather expensive.

Cutting tools can be used not only for cutting masks and stencils but also for scraping out attractive highlights. Round blades are particularly suitable for this purpose. With a bit of practice you should be able to scrape fine lines as well as wider areas. If you do scrape, however, make sure that your illustration board is adequate: a firm, smooth surface is best.

5.5 Choice of Paint

There is a tremendous variety of different paints. For the purpose of the airbrush we can classify them roughly into sprayable and non-sprayable. Here we are obviously only concerned with the former.

A paint is sprayable if it can be thinned down so much that it will go through the nozzle of an airbrush. In fact, it should have the consistency of ordinary milk.

Another criterion is the way in which it will react to the airbrush itself. Never use fast-drying paints because of the danger of blockage. Also, avoid paints that become very hard once they are dry because they could cause irreparable damage inside your airbrush. Some paints even contain rather aggressive substances that might attack the metal.

Nevertheless, the choice is still so great that, to make reasonable distinctions, we shall have to form further subgroups. In the context of this book, we shall distinguish between pigment-based paints and non-pigment paints, with each group being divided into those which are water-resistant when they have dried and those which are not. To avoid unfairness, I shall refrain from quoting brandnames. It is likely that I would forget quite a few and that might lead to hard feelings. Instead, I shall discuss a number of different types and their characteristic features.

Let us begin with the water-resistant ones. A pigment-based paint is a coloured substance that can be organic, mineral or synthetic in nature. It is very fine and swims in a solvent. Most of them are opaque, i.e. they cover the surface on which they are sprayed. Only a very small number are slightly transparent.

Nevertheless, they can still be used for glazing. They just have to be thinned down a lot. When the paint is applied to the surface, the individual particles cover the ground completely, but they are so far apart that the space between them is still visible. The more layers of colour are applied, however, the more the paint will become opaque again.

Once the paint has dried, it cannot be dissolved again, at least not by means of water or more paint. There are some pigment-based paints, however, which respond to special solvents when they are dry. This group includes oil-based paints and acrylics. The former can be thinned down with turpentine or other suitable substances while still wet, while acrylics can even be treated with water at this stage.

The group of paints which are not water-resistant includes water-colour, gouache and tempera. All these can be thinned down with water. The airbrush is the only tool that allows you to apply several layers of paint without dissolving the existing one – something that would be impossible with an ordinary paintbrush.

All pigment-based paints are extremely light-resistant, oil and acrylic more so than gouache or water-colour. Unfortunately, however, they do tend to solidify into lumps and clog up the nozzle. In particular, this can affect the tip of the needle and therefore also the sprayed result. The only way to avoid this is to clean the airbrush regularly.

Non-pigment paints are considerably less problematic in this respect, which makes them ideally suited for the airbrush. However, they are anything but fade-proof. If an illustration is to be used in printing, this does not matter too much, because the photographic and lithographic processes will conserve the picture "for posterity" anyway.

Non-pigment paints are completely transparent and the most widely known are glaze, ink and also some types of India ink. Everything underneath them can be seen as if through glass.

Colour shades that are superimposed influence the ones below. This means that you can mix the most saturated and intensive hues – better, in fact, than with pigment-based paints.

A final word about possible health hazards. Most studio paints are neither toxic nor otherwise dangerous to your health.

Nevertheless, you should always read carefully the specifications of the manufacturer and, if necessary, wear a face mask or install an extractor hood.

On the other hand, though, they do force you to avoid mistakes completely. Not even the slightest misplaced drop of paint can be covered up if you are using pigment-free paint. Protein-based paint and ink are not water-resistant when they are dry, while some types of India ink can be. All these paints can be thinned down with ordinary water.

6.1 Definition

Let us now take a look at the different clients who are interested in airbrushed illustrations. At this point, I would like to define the expression "airbrush illustration" a little more clearly. It is very rare for an artist to use nothing but an airbrush, for he makes equal use of tools such as pencils, pens and paintbrushes. Nevertheless, it is the airbrush which allows him to produce such even and finely measured lines and contours that the final result looks almost photographic. The illustrations which I have summarized under the heading "airbrush" could therefore also be called "photographic realism".

6.2 Who Needs Illustrations?

So who needs and, above all, who can afford photographic realism? The type of picture that such a client wants is of its very nature a very time-consuming affair, which means that it simply cannot be cheap. It may be well worth its price, but it is still rather costly. Unfortunately, customers tend to see the price in absolute terms rather than relating it to the amount of time it takes to produce a piece of work. Even when they do see our work in realistic terms, they still have to make the same calculations in their own business that we do in ours, i.e. they expect a sensible relationship between the price of an illustration and its use. If the hairdresser round the corner wanted your service, he would be the exception.

Without wanting to claim comprehensiveness, I have made a small list of potential clients. The order is completely random and does not imply any value judgements.

First, there are the manufacturers of technical products such as aeroplanes, cars, motor-bikes, machines, cameras, radios, television sets, computers, etc. The products which they make and sell need to be explained not only verbally but also visually, and this cannot always be done with photographs. For instance, think of the 'ghosting' or 'exploding' techniques.

The pharmaceutical industry forms another group of clients. The effects and applications of their products can be illustrated very nicely.

Then there are architects and manufacturers of prefab buildings who often need pictures of things that only exist on the drawing-board. It is undoubtedly cheaper and more worthwhile to illustrate the prototype of a new prefab than to actually build it.

All these clients have one thing in common: the very development of their products costs enormous amounts of money. And if the turnover can be increased by means of good, sales-promoting illustrations, then the price which is paid for them is reasonable when compared to the money that had to be put into the development of the product.

6.3 Advertising Agencies as Agents and Clients

There is another point which clients of these proportions have in common, i.e. they are hardly ever direct customers of the artist, but have contacted him via an agent. After all, which illustrator would be capable of dealing with budgets going into six or seven figures? You would need a whole army of staff – and once you've got them to cope with, that'll be the end of the peace and quiet which you need for good illustrations.

This means that the art directors and art buyers of advertising agencies will continue to be the people we have to deal with most of the time. They are the ones who have to be informed about the range of services we offer. Thoroughly and regularly. Do not hesitate to get on their nerves a little – it will make them all the more willing to get rid of you by giving you a little trial commission.

Once you have your foot in the door of an agency, other commissions will soon follow suit. It is a branch of industry which is smaller than it seems, and if you produce good work will soon become known elsewhere.

But this also applies to bad illustrators, and they become known even more quickly. An illustrator is expected to produce perfect work. There can be no doubt about that. And woe to the artist who produces a piece of slipshod work! The agencies will remember him forever. And they will start gossiping about it all over the place. So do be careful. It is better to put in the odd night-shift than to hand in a picture that is poor in quality.

You should also consider night-shifts when you are faced with difficult deadlines. Unless you are actually in intensive care with a heart attack, you should never exceed a deadline. It might have the same effect as the heart attack.

I was deliberately emphatic on my last two points because they really are extremely important. All the colleagues with whom I have discussed these topics agree. And why should you repeat mistakes and pay for them dearly if others have done that before you?

On the whole, however, agencies are quite pleasant to work with. The artist may not get very many opportunities to give rein to his own creativity, but at least not much can go wrong. Even delicate areas such as user's fees and copyright are normally taken care of without discussion by most agencies.

6.4 Artists' Agencies and Representatives

Another way in which commissions can be obtained is through individual agents and representatives. Artists have their agents in the same way that sportsmen have their managers. The relationship is in fact very similar. To show the function of an agent, I interviewed MARGARETHE HUBAUER, who has been an agent in Hamburg for a number of years.

6.5 Interview with MARGARETHE HUBAUER

MICHAEL METTE: Can you just give us a brief idea of what you do?

MARGARETHE HUBAUER: "Give you an idea", yes – but I'm not sure about the "briefly". I represent a large number of internationally famous illustrators who do commission work for the advertising industry and the press, for book and record publishers. But I also act on behalf of a number of illustrators who are not very well-known yet, but whose works I think are extraordinarily interesting and promising. That's my personal opinion, but it's based on years of experience.

I act as an intermediary between two worlds which still don't know each other very well: the world of artistic illustrations and the world of commerce. Based on a short and precise interview, I establish the contact between a client and the illustrator whose style and technique are most suitable for a particular task.

This task is then carried out, and I accompany it as an intermediary, adviser and often – especially with commissions from abroad – quite literally as a translator.

At the same time I try to initiate all kinds of activities that will help these two worlds to get to know each other better, for example by organizing regular exhibitions of the works of the artists I represent.

My aim is to put the idea of "art for commerce" into practice. There should more of an awareness of how illustrations can contribute to commercial success.

METTE: How does an artist who is interested actually contact you or one of your colleagues?

HUBAUER: All he has to do is give me a ring and send me a few samples.

METTE: What do you expect from an illustrator you represent? What kind of conditions are there?

HUBAUER: There are a number of points, some of them objective, others subjective. The most important one is that he should be skilful and produce good quality. If he is a younger artist, there should at least be some recognizable talent and the willingness to improve further.

Secondly, the style of the illustrator has to be suitable for commercial use. He has to keep to deadlines and he must be able occasionally to put the client's ideas first, rather than his own.

Finally, there should be a minimum of personal sympathy between myself and the illustrator.

METTE: What are the reasons why an illustrator turns to you?

HUBAUER: Probably the idea that he will get more commissions and more interesting ones – and that is often the case. And of course it is a well-known fact that most artists loathe admin and negotiating terms. These are jobs which an agent can do for them.

METTE: When you come to an agreement with an illustrator, you set up a contract. Could such an artist then still take on commissions independently, without you?

HUBAUER: That depends. If an illustrator has been in business for quite a while, you cannot tell him to stop working with his old clients directly. If somebody is new to the profession, however, I suggest an exclusive contract, because it would be too difficult for him to work out all the time which job comes from whom and which one doesn't.

METTE: So you've got your core of illustrators. How do you get the clients?

HUBAUER: Well, I've been doing this for twelve years and over the years a core of clients has built up, of course. Also, I take my artists' portfolios to the advertising agencies regularly and I hand out a calendar every year with samples which has become quite popular by now.

The best advertisement – as in everything – is word-of-mouth propaganda by satisfied customers.

METTE: What kind of clients are there? Just agencies, or are there also direct customers among them? Do you ever get private clients at all who might want illustrations?

HUBAUER: Mainly agencies. But there are also some direct customers and freelance advertising consultants. I hardly ever get any private customers because they don't normally know about me.

METTE: Word-of-mouth propaganda. But surely that can't be enough for the right people to find out about your services and your artists. What can an agent do in terms of advertising for himself and self-promotion? And, secondly: what do you actually do?

HUBAUER: I could do a lot if I wanted to and have done so in the past. For instance, direct mailing campaigns to a selected number of clients. Of course whole branches of industry could be virtually inundated with bumph – but I don't think much of that, which doesn't mean of course that it might not be quite effective.

As I said before, the most important thing really is the quality of the work. Our calendar has been very successful, too. It has already made a name for itself in dominant circles as "The Illustrator's Calendar" and is often used as a basis for choosing an artist.

Another promotion job which I started in spring 1986 are regular exhibitions at our new gallery "Art for Commerce".

METTE: But things like that cost money. I assume you finance them by agreeing on an agency fee, a certain percentage on a piece of work which you agree on beforehand. How much do you charge? And do the illustrators have to pay for their own advertising? You know, a membership fee or something like that.

HUBAUER: Depending on the country, the fee can vary between 20 and 30 percent. As for the artist's own advertising, this is probably handled differently by different agents. My artists contribute to the cost of the calendar. Otherwise this project would be impossible. I have never actually heard of membership fees in our business.

METTE: There's one other point I'd like to raise, i.e. the business side of the commissions you hand out. Most artists tend to be somewhat naïve when it comes to business. Do you help them in any way? And if so, how?

HUBAUER: As soon as an artist has been given a particular job, we send off a confirmation with all the details about payment, user's rights, the deadline, ownership of the original, etc.

But the final invoice goes through our agency again. Occasionally we negotiate additional payments.

METTE: Finally, I'd like to ask you the same question as the illustrators. What do you think about the future of the airbrush? And what about photographic realism?

HUBAUER: Personally, I think there is no point in photographic realism unless a subject cannot be photographed. Otherwise, I believe that a personal hallmark – even with the airbrush – is far more attractive. Pure airbrush works have a touch of coldness and smoothness about them and cannot be used everywhere.

The best thing would be if every artist were to develop his own technique, his own style. Following the perfection which has been reached recently, particularly by the Japanese, there has been a marked tendency towards more freedom.

METTE: Thank you very much.

GILDA BELIN is undoubtedly one of the most active women in a job that tends to be dominated by men. Her career sounds almost American with all the vairous stages she has been going through.

Together with her partner, FRED-JÜRGEN ROGNER, who is also an illustrator and represented in this book, she lives in the South of France and works for the international market.

I discussed with them one of the most critical aspects of our hard business, i.e. copyright. GILDA BELIN's works have sold worldwide and it seems to me that her comments on this subject are worth a small chapter.

GILDA BELIN: We've lost count of the number of solicitors we've employed. In fact, we've got three law-suits going on at the moment, two in France and one in the States.

At first my blood pressure used to rise whenever I saw one of my pictures being used by someone who hadn't bought. Now I am a lot calmer about it, but also harder.

FRED-JÜRGEN ROGNER: You can't imagine how trivial these things often are. One particular case in Germany involves no more than 360 German marks (about £120). And it's been going on for about two years.

BELIN: It's really a matter of principle. But we've already spent several thousand marks on solicitor's fees.

METTE: Do you mind if I ask you what this case is about?

ROGNER: Our works were exhibited at an art gallery and one of them went missing. When we investigated the matter, it suddenly turned out that it had been sold.

BELINS: That wasn't the worst thing. We agreed with the art gallery that they could keep the costs and should then pay the balance, i.e. the amount we mentioned earlier on. It was up to us to prove that the original had been sold.

ROGNER: The art dealer was annoyed because we took legal action immediately. We had just moved to England at the time and he said he couldn't find us anywhere.

We had tried to contact him twice before then. When we didn't succeed, we asked our solicitor to act on our behalf. It may well have been a series of misunderstandings.

Still, he kept refusing to pay. This is how a law-suit can start quite easily.

In a copyright case the artist is usually the weakest party. That's why such things are often swept under the carpet.

METTE: But artists are rather naïve in legal matters, aren't they?

BELIN: They are at the beginning. And so were we. But as time goes on, you become more experienced. We do after all have to live on our art – and if it gets stolen from us, we have to defend ourselves.

ROGNER: Very much to be recommended! Because if more of us insisted on getting our rights, then fewer people would try to take them away from us.

BELIN: A few years ago I had a case against a well-known cosmetics firm. One day I found one of my illustrations on one of their posters. And I was absolutely sure that I had not made it for that client or that particular purpose.

I turned to their advertising department and was told the picture had been made by an illustrator on their own staff. So I threatened them with legal action. The firm immediately yielded and offered me 2000 marks (appr. £500 at the time), but I thought that big companies like that should know that it is wrong to steal other people's work. So I rejected the offer and started to take action.

METTE: How much did you get in the end?

BELIN: Three times as much and the solicitor's fees of course.

METTE: Good for you! It's a pity not all colleagues follow your example.

ROGNER: Well, there are a number of reasons that make you think twice before going to a solicitor. The cosmetics firm Gilda told you about will probably never be a client of ours. They're rather peeved now.

So the question is whether one should take legal action against a faithful client. This is a rather complicated issue.

BELIN: It really is difficult for an individual illustrator to take action against a potential customer. But in my experience it doesn't pay to be too generous with copyright. One day you reach the stage where you've achieved a lot in your life but you haven't been getting anything for it.

METTE: How could all this have been avoided?

BELIN: Our worst mistake was that we were too credulous. The first illustration we sold to America went to a big publishing company which printed postcards. We were really proud of ourselves and thought we had made it – and then we started waiting for the hard dollars.

ROGNER: Which never came. But we did see our pictures again. In the form of postcards, just as we had agreed, but published by the wrong company.

We were already living in England by that time. And it was a British publishing house that had printed our postcards, not an American one. It turned out that they had bought our illustrations – including all the rights – from our American client.

METTE: You mean you didn't specify user's rights when you wrote your invoice?

BELIN: That's just it, we didn't. We just kept thinking of all the other work we'd be getting.

ROGNER: So we went to see a British solicitor, who then filed a lawsuit. At that point we got our first cold shower in copyright matters. Before anything could happen, we were asked to put £1000 on the table.

Our solicitor engaged the help of a partner firm in the States, but it was exactly the same there. First the money, then the law-suit.

METTE: And all that simply because your bill did not include enough information.

BELIN: Of course we have learnt our lesson. It was so expensive we were unlikely to forget it again. Ever since then we have always insisted on absolutely water-tight contracts and clearly defined user's rights.

ROGNER: But things like this still happen. After our first American adventure, though, we always won whenever we were in the right.

Following page: "Music Lover"
Intended use: poster
Format: 55 x 70 cm
Ground: Schoellershammer hard board
Colours: gouache
Airbrush: Conopois
Commissioned by Mustang Jeans

Left: "Call Me"
Intended use: calendar, greetings card
Format: 86 x 60 cm
Ground: Schoellershammer hard board
Colours: India ink and gouache
Airbrushes: Conopois and Grafo

Page after next: "Fitness"
Intended use: poster
Format: 37 x 51 cm
Ground: Schoellershammer hard board
Colours: gouache
Airbrush: Conopois
Commissioned by Verkerke

gilda belin

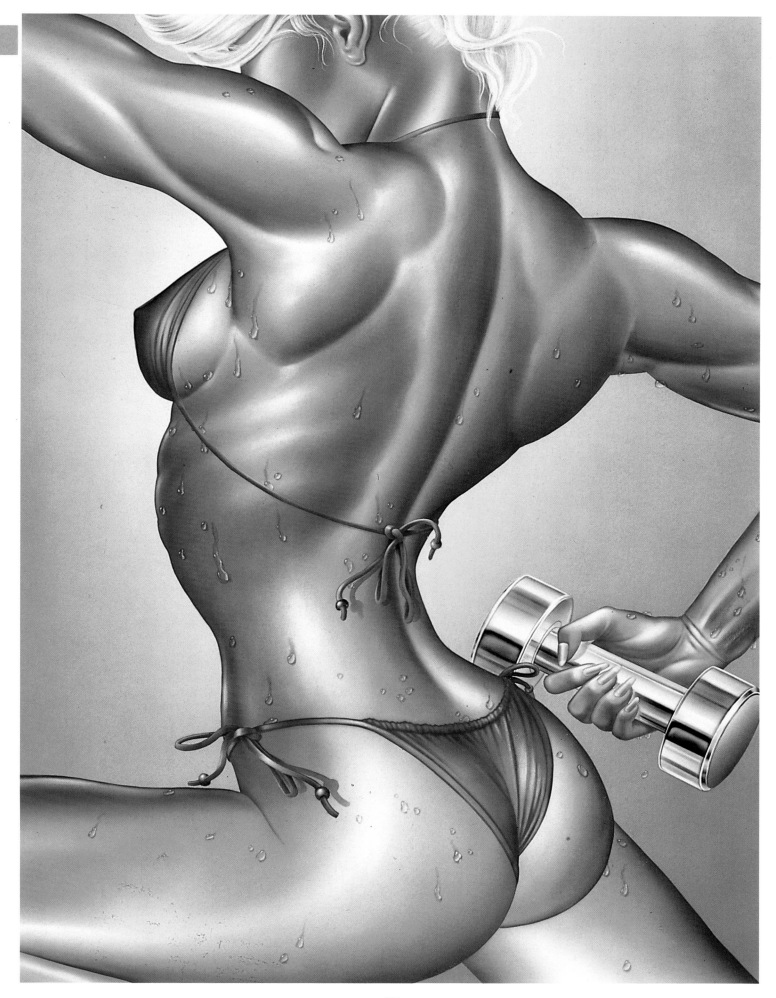

45

BELIN ROGNER ARTISTS

Right: "Fair Lady"
Intended use: magazine cover for "AVANTGARDE"
Format: 50 x 70 cm
Ground: Schoellershammer hard board
Colours: gouache
Airbrush: Conopois
Commissioned by Wenton

Below: Untitled
Intended use: poster
Format: 50 x 70 cm
Ground: Schoellershammer hard board
Colours: gouache
Airbrush: Conopois

Right, top: "Vespa"
Intended use: poster and carrier bag
Format: 60 x 75 cm
Ground: Schoellershammer hard board
Colours: gouache
Airbrush: Conopois

Right, large picture: "Back from the Beach"
Intended use: postcard
Format: 60 x 50 cm
Ground: Schoellershammer hard board
Colours: acrylic and gouache
Airbrushes: Conopois and Grafo
Commissioned by: Verkerke

Right, below: "New York in Winter"
Intended use: postcard
Format: 40 x 50 cm
Ground: Schoellershammer hard board
Colours: gouache
Airbrush: Conopois
Commissioned by: Verkerke

©Belin

BELIN ROGNER ARTISTS

Below: "Mind Games"
Intended use: magazine and book illustration
Format: 40 x 40 cm
Ground: Schoellershammer hard board
Colours: gouache and India ink

Airbrush: Conopois
Commissioned by: Penthouse, Goldmann, Zwarte Beetjes

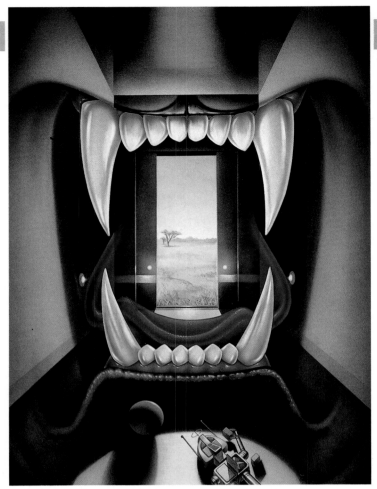

Left: "In the Gallery"
Intended use: poster and magazine cover
Format: 50 x 70 cm
Ground: Schoellershammer hard board
Colours: gouache
Airbrush: Conopois
Commissioned by: Mustang Jeans

Below: "Autokino"
Intended use: poster
Format: 60 x 75 cm
Ground: Schoellershammer hard board
Colours: gouache
Airbrush: Conopois
Commissioned by: Mustang Jeans

Left, top: "The Children's Room"
Intended use: science fiction illustration
Format: 40 x 40 cm
Ground: Schoellershammer hard board
Colours: gouache and India ink
Airbrush: Conopois
Commissioned by: Motor Magazine

Left, below: "No Fear of Death"
Intended use: magazine illustration
Format: 60 x 50 cm
Ground: Schoellershammer hard board
Colours: gouache and India ink
Airbrush: Conopois
Commissioned by: Playboy

Left: "Untitled"
Intended use: anniversary edition for author of a bestseller
Format: 80 x 75 cm
Ground: Schoellershammer hard board
Colours: acrylic, gouache, pastel crayon and coloured pencils
Airbrush: Conopois
Commissioned by: Goldmann Verlag

Right: "Room No. 3"
Intended use: independent work, used later in Penthouse
Format: 60 x 50 cm
Ground: Schoellershammer hard board
Colours: acrylic
Airbrush: Conopois

Below: "The Limits of the Universe"
Intended use: magazine illustration
Format: 60 x 50 cm
Ground: Schoellershammer hard board
Colours: gouache
Airbrush: Conopois
Commissioned by: Playboy

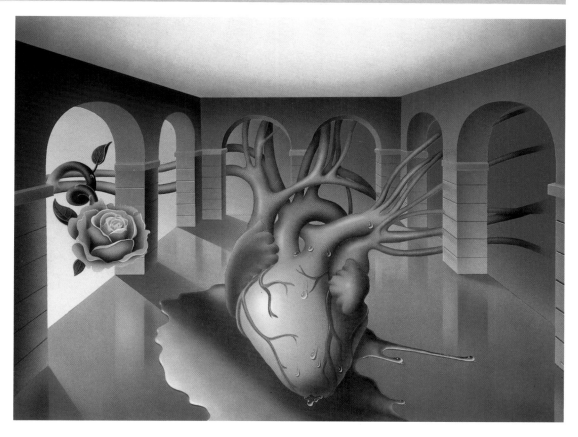

UERRINO BOATTO lives and works in Venice, more precisely in an industrial suburb of Venice called Mestre. He was born in 1949 and has been one of the best-known and most prolific artists on the airbrush scene.

When I met him at his studio, which is also where he lives, there was classical music playing in the background and a half-finished piece of work on his table.

He had been working on a pair of training shoes shown in front of a tiled wall, the final version of which can be seen in this book.

Although he was working hard to meet a deadline, he still managed to find enough time for our interview. Thank you very much, Guerrino.

METTE: When did you actually start making illustrations?

BOATTO: I started very early, when I was still at school. And as soon as I finished school, I joined the Academy of Art in Venice, where I continued to learn to paint and draw. My subject was graphic design because I wanted to be a graphic designer.

When I got my diploma, I soon found a job at a small agency, where I worked as a graphic designer.

METTE: That was here in Venice, was it?

BOATTO: Yes. I really learnt everything right from the beginning. Drawing, typesetting and things like that. And so I gradually acquired more and more experience and concentrated on designing, particularly layouts.

METTE: When did you first come across the airbrush?

BOATTO: It was at that time. I had always been inter-ested in all kind of techniques. One day I saw a small airbrushed picture so I just kept on studying until I knew what the technique was all about.

After some searching I even found a shop where they sold airbrushes, and so I bought my first airbrush. However, at the beginning I could only use it for backgrounds and very simple subjects. I had no experience. Most of my works at that time were still structured very diagrammatically, with relatively simple forms, shad-ows and contours.

METTE: You obviously didn't stop at that stage. Where and how did you gather all your experience?

BOATTO: I used to learn most when I tried to analyse and imitate airbrushed pictures which had been made by other people. And I was always very consistent and extremely patient about it. As time went on my skills gradually improved. This phase lasted about two years. And then a friend of mine went to San Francisco and told me that the airbrush technique was taught at college there.

So I went to San Francisco too and studied there for a few years. Back in Venice, I began to work as a free-lance illustrator. I've been working with a Milan agent since 1982. Since then I've only painted pictures and I haven't done any graphic design work at all.

METTE: Do you always do your illustrations on your own, Guerrino, or do you sometimes ask a colleague, for instance that friend you mentioned, to join you on a project?

BOATTO: Yes, I have done a few pictures together with a friend in the past. But I do most of them on my own.

METTE: Do you ever find the time and the inclination to do a piece of work just for the fun of it?

BOATTO: No, I don't. I've had the good – or bad – fortune that my agent has been inundating me with commercial jobs so such an extent that there there's never been any time left for that sort of thing.

METTE: How long will you be able to work so intensively and so hard? Have you ever thought about that?

BOATTO: Not very often. Just as years ago I couldn't imagine that I'd be an illustrator one day, I haven't got a very clear idea of my future now.

Sometimes I think that computer graphics might be interesting. But thoughts like that are still rather vague. For the time being I'm happy with things as they are.

METTE: Where do you get your ideas from?

BOATTO: Usually look at photographs. I've collected quite a lot over the years. Sometimes I get reference photos from my clients, sometimes I take them myself and sometimes I work straight from the original subject.

METTE: Do you start with sketches?

BOATTO: Yes, always. I start off with small pencil sketches which I transfer onto tracing-paper. Then I trace it onto the illustration-board. To be on the safe side, I keep the sketch so that I can always refer back to it later on.

METTE: And then you cover your board with masking film?

BOATTO: Yes, for the first colours. I usually work in such a way that the background shades and basic colours are sprayed in different stages. This means that I need several masks.

I find it easier to do just the first layer with self-adhesive film, then I usually use transparent acetate which I hold down to the surface. This makes the edges a little less sharp, a bit softer.

Then I work out the structures and nuances with a paint-brush.

METTE: How long does it take you to make an illustration like these training shoes?

BOATTO: The actual airbrushing, i.e. the background and the basic shapes, takes about a day. And then it takes me another two or three days until the finer nuances have been worked out.

METTE: Which airbrushes do you use?

BOATTO: Well, I've got a Paasche V-1, two IWATA HP-B's, an IWATA HP-BE1 and an Olympos for larger areas. Normally I only use one for each illustration. There's one thing which I think is very important: as soon as I've finished a job, I clean my airbrush and I don't put it together again until the next time I use it.

METTE: I see you use mainly non-transparent colours. What kind of paint do you prefer?

BOATTO: I nearly always use acrylic, both for spraying and painting. Just occasionally I use gouache. I always thin the paint down so much that it is transparent, though after a few layers it becomes opaque again. This enables me to finish off the dark parts of an illustration first and to get a better idea of the contrasts.

METTE: Which ground do you normally do your illustrations on?

BOATTO: I always use Schoeller illustration line board, you know, the thick kind with several layers stuck together. My formats are usually around 50 x 60 cms, which can't really be scanned directly by the lithographer so he just has to make slides first.

This format is a lot safer for my originals. It has happened in the past that the litho people took the surface off smaller illustrations so that they couldn't be used again.

METTE: What actually happens to your originals?

BOATTO: I'd always like to have them back, but that's not always possible. Some originals are now hanging in the offices of my clients.

METTE: When you get a job to do, what is the procedure? I imagine you get it from your private agent or an agency ...

BOATTO: ... usually with a ready-made layout.

METTE: Does it ever happen that you have to or you're allowed to work out the layout yourself?

BOATTO: Very rarely. The majority of the illustrations I make are for advertising campaigns and come from agencies, so they've already been agreed on by their art or creative directors and the clients.

Before I start working on the original, all I do is discuss the illustration with a contact person at the agency. That way I can be pretty sure that it won't be necessary to add corrections later on.

METTE: One final question: is there a future for the airbrush technique?

BOATTO: I'm absolutely convinced there is. One day, perhaps, the computer will be able to do a few jobs for us – but even a computer can never be better than the person who operates it. And there are many areas, especially when you're illustrating relatively freely, which can probably never be handled by a machine.

Above: Untitled
Intended use: calendar illustration
Format: 50 x 70 cm
Ground: Schoellershammer hard board
Colours: Liquitex
Airbrushes: Paasche V1 and Olympos
Commissioned by: Fiat

Right, top: Untitled
Intended use: illustration on wrapping paper
Format: 35 x 50 cm
Ground: Schoellershammer hard board
Colours: Liquitex
Airbrushes: Paasche V1 and VL1
Commissioned by: Dalco

Right: Untitled
Intended use: advertising
Format: 50 x 80 cm
Ground: Schoellershammer hard board
Colours: Liquitex
Airbrushes: Paasche V1 and VL1
Commissioned by: Nava

Following page, top: Untitled
Intended use: calendar illustration
Format: 50 x 70 cm
Ground: Schoellershammer hard board
Colours: Liquitex
Airbrush: Paasche V1
Commissioned by: Fiat

Following page, below: Untitled
Intended use: advertising
Format: 50 x 70 cm
Ground: Schoellershammer hard board
Colours: Liquitex
Airbrushes: Paasche V1 and IWATA HP-SB
Commissioned by: Pirelli

Page 59:
Intended use: advertising
Format: 50 x 70 cm
Ground: Schoellershammer hard board
Colours: Liquitex
Airbrushes: Paasche V1 and IWATA HP-SB
Commissioned by: Pirelli

Far left, top: Untitled
Intended use: advertising
Format: 50 x 70 cm
Ground: Schoellershammer hard board
Colours: Liquitex
Airbrush: Paasche V1
Commissioned by: Ford

Left: Untitled
Intended use: advertising
Format: 50 x 70 cm
Ground: Schoellershammer hard board
Airbrush: Paasche V1
Commissioned by: Honeywell

Above: Untitled
Intended use: book illustration
Format: 40 x 60 cm
Ground: Schoellershammer hard board
Colours: Liquitex
Airbrushes: Paasche V1 and VL1
Commissioned by: Venice Institute of Art

61

NORBERT CAMES was born in Mönchengladbach, West Germany, on 1st September, 1953. When he finished school, he began to train as a lithographer. Then he was employed as a draughtsman by a big agency. It was during this time that he made his first smaller illustrations for his employer. These were black-and-white at first, and later coloured. He has been working as a freelance illustrator since 1981.

A brief glance at NORBERT CAMES's curriculum vitae reveals that he never did any academic studies in the traditional sense of the word. As soon as he knew what he wanted to be, he aimed at teaching himself. And even his choice of training place was geared towards this aim. The lithographic techniques and skills which he acquired during that period formed a solid basis for the way in which he now works.

But in spite of all this careful planning, NORBERT CAMES had to do a lot of improvising during his first few years as a freelance artist. He himself says that the work was "tricky" and quotes a few examples in the interview.

METTE: You mentioned that you installed your first darkroom under the sitting-room table. Were there any other ways in which you had to improvise to make ends meet?

NORBERT CAMES: I did indeed have to compromise, not only because of the furniture in my flat, but also where I actually worked. At the beginning I had no pro-

fessional studio, and everything I needed had to be stored in the smallest possible space. So I had my darkroom under the table, covered with a black blanket so that I could develop my rolls of film.

Large-format airbrush pictures were another tricky affair. I just couldn't do them at all in our sitting-room. So I built a wind shelter on the balcony with a few wooden beams and some sheets of plastic. Wearing a thick jacket, I used to work there even in winter, spraying some of my best pictures.

METTE: When did you actually start using the airbrush in your artwork?

CAMES: I first came across it when I was still training to be a lithographer. I was asked to airbrush a sphere. Later, when I was working for the agency, I saw airbrushed pictures more frequently and soon came to realize that I somehow had to come to terms with the medium. At first I practised with an instrument that belonged to the agency, but soon decided to buy my own.

METTE: Apart from your training, where else could a person learn to use the airbrush in those days? Were there seminars, books, etc.?

CAMES: Not as far as I know. Like most of my colleagues, I've always been sort of an individualist. Illustrations are hardly ever created by a team. And so I acquired all my airbrush skills myself, following the trial-and-error principle. After a while I learnt to design all my works – even my experiments – in my mind first before putting them into practice. I believe that it is really vital for a good illustrator to be able to do this.

METTE: That certainly requires a lot of patience. How long do you think it takes before one can see the first concrete result?

CAMES: There's no general answer to that question. But it can be disastrous if you've spent too little time on all the preliminaries. Everybody has to learn this the hard way. If there is one thing that no illustrator should do, then that is to hand in a piece of work which has been patched up. No matter how close the deadline may be, if I've made a mistake then that means that I've got to start again. I just cannot afford to risk my reputation which has taken me years of hard work to build up.

On one occasion I had to start again half-way through the time I was given. It cost me several nights. I just had to do the job within half the time and I was expected to produce the same quality! This is really horrible, and I gladly spend a lot of time and energy on the preliminaries if I can avoid such disasters.

METTE: Yes, it can happen that you've been working on an illustration for ten days, and "all" you've got to do is to add the highlights. How does it feel deep down?

CAMES: I'm no longer afraid of it, simply because I've been successful so many times. I do of course take my precautions: I take a piece of black hard board and regulate the air pressure very closely to the spot where the paint is supposed to hit the ground and then move the airbrush in that direction by a few millimetres only.

METTE: Do you develop such tricks whenever you need them or do they come to you by chance? During the preliminaries or the actual work on the illustration itself?

CAMES: Usually during the preliminary stages. It happens almost every day that I think of something new. For instance, I might suddenly get the rolling-pin from the kitchen or a comb glued up with paint – very often these tricks are a matter of pure chance, but in most cases I actually have to think of something.

METTE: What sort of material do you use? You know, stencils, masking film etc.

CAMES: I use everything! Because I think there's no such thing as the ideal material. Everything has its strong and weak points. I do of course have my preferences by now; for instance, I love tempera colours and I always mix them myself. But the next job may force me to use glaze.

METTE: Do you have any preferences with regard to subject style?

CAMES: Well, I've never specialized in any particular subject. Everything that cannot be photographed usually needs to be airbrushed. And that's what my job is all about. There's one exception, though. I used to make film posters with a lot of action in them but now I feel that I don't want to paint pictures with nothing but people in them. If I've been working on several still-lifes or objects, I find it rather difficult to work on a picture of people moving about.

METTE: What I would find interesting is where you get your ideas from and what do you do with them?

CAMES: I've been trying for years to have as many pictures in my head as I can, so that I can use them whenever I need them. Also, I've built up quite an extensive archive which has been quite helpful as a source of information. After all, who knows by heart how many parts the shell of a crayfish consists of? Sometimes you even have to buy your model. The other day, for instance, I was asked to paint a pike, so I just had to buy the "original".

METTE: Did you actually put it on the table?

CAMES: Yes.

METTE: Was it still there after three days?

CAMES: I took a few good polaroid photos and then put the pike in the freezer. The photos were adequate enough for the rough outlines. But whenever I needed details, such as the scales and the eyes, I had to unfreeze it. The smell wasn't always very pleasant.

METTE: Finally, as an illustrator, what is your view of the future of the airbrush?

CAMES: I can't imagine illustrations without the airbrush any longer. There are certain areas where it's simply impossible to achieve perfection without it. After the present boom there may of course be a trend-reversal one day, but the airbrush will never disappear completely. I must say, though, that with a realistic subject you sometimes only use the airbrush for about forty percent of the picture, and the rest is still done with more traditional tools, such as a pen, a pencil and a paintbrush.

NORBERT CAMES

Left, top: "Spoon of a Spinner"
Intended use: teaching plates for anglers
Format: 8.5 x 19.6 cm
Ground: illustration line board
Colours: water–colour
Airbrush: EFBE B1, hard
Commissioned by: Hospo Verlag, Cologne

Left, middle: "Angler's Winch"
Intended use: teaching plates for anglers
Format: 15 x 19.5 cm
Ground: illustration line board
Colours: water-colour
Airbrush: EFBE B1, hard
Commissioned by: Hospo Verlag, Cologne

Left, bottom: "Spoon of a Spinner"
Intended use: teaching plates for anglers
Format: 6.5 x 21 cm
Ground: illustration line board
Colours: water-colour
Airbrush: EFBE B1, hard
Commissioned by: Hospo Verlag, Cologne

Below: "Pike"
Format: 45 x 18 cm
Ground: illustration line board
Colours: water-colour
Airbrush: EFBE B1, hard
Commissioned by: Deutscher Angelsportverein

Above: "The Hunter"
Intended use: art poster
Format: 50 x 80 cm
Ground: wood
Colours: Liquitex acrylic and India ink
Airbrush: EFBE B1, hard

Right: Untitled
Intended use: art poster
Format: 48 x 56 cm
Ground: illustration line board
Colours: water-colour and glaze
Airbrush: EFBE B1, hard

NORBERT CAMES

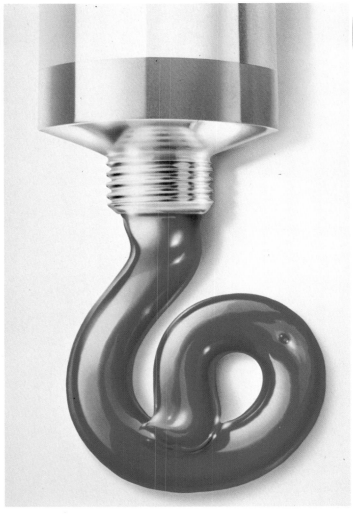

Left, top: Untitled
Intended use: technical illustration
Format: 40 x 40 cm
Ground: illustration line board
Colours: Schmincke Aerocolor
Airbrush: EFBE B1, hard
Commissioned by: Zeiss Ikon

Above: Untitled
Intended use: cover illustration
Format: 40 x 30 cm
Ground: illustration line board
Colours: acrylic
Airbrush: EFBE B1, hard
Commissioned by: Art Director's
Index

Left: "Tin with Tomatoes"
Format: 32 x 40 cm
Ground: illustration line board
Colours: acrylic
Airbrush: EFBE B1, hard
Commissioned by: Weissblech
Industrie

Far right: "The Elephant Man"
Format: 65 x 90 cm
Ground: Wood
Colours: tempera
Airbrush: EFBE B1, hard

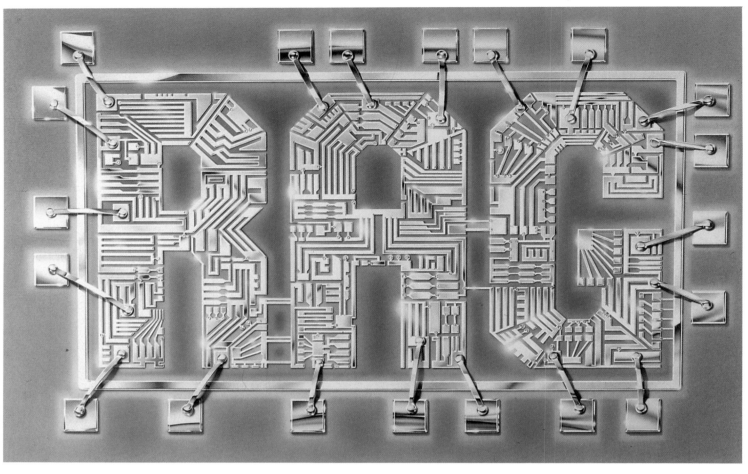

Above: Untitled
Intended use: advertising
Format: 50 x 80 cm
Ground: illustration line board
Colours: acrylic and glaze
Airbrush: EFBE B1, hard
Commissioned by: Ruhrkohle AG

Below: "Pfanni"
Format: 30 x 39 cm
Ground: illustration line board
Colours: water-colour
Airbrush: EFBE B1, hard
Commissioned by: Pfanni

Above: Untitled
Intended use: part of an anniversary logos
Format: 50 x 50 cm
Ground: illustration line board
Colours: Liquitex acrylic and Dr. Martin water-colours
Airbrush: EFBE B1, hard
Commissioned by: Horten AG

Below: Untitled
Intended use: advertising
Format: 31 x 40 cm
Ground: illustration line board
Colours: Liquitex acrylic
Airbrush: EFBE B1, hard
Commissioned by: Grey, Düsseldorf

Above: "Tyres"
Intended use: advertising campaign
Format: 42 x 80 cm
Ground: illustration line board
Colours: water-colour
Airbrush: EFBE B1, hard
Commissioned by: Fulda-Reifen

Left: "Fruit"
Format: 28 x 36 cm
Ground: illustration line board
Colours: water-colour
Airbrush: EFBE

MARC ERICKSEN lives quite close to Silicon valley, in San Fransisco, California. It is quite obvious from his art that he has been infuenced both by the place where he lives and also by computer technology. His pictures are dominated by strong, clear colours and a large number of electronic technical motifs.

This is his own account of how he achieved such glowing results:

"I start almost every job with a 'scribble-in'. I sit down with my client and, using one – or if necessary – several drawings, I try to come to an agreement about his ideas and mine. Sometimes we end up having real discussions. However, we always get to the point very nicely.

In the next step I make two or three pencil sketches, which are still rather rough. I usually work with smaller formats, about 5 by 10 inches. One of these scribbles eventually serves as the basis for the final version.

The first colour comes into play in the next step. At this stage I'm still working very roughly with markers, and I try to make things as easy for myself as I can, simulating the airbrush effect as well as possible by using other techniques and materials. After these preliminaries – provided my client has given his blessing – I start working on the first more elaborate drawing. This is done with ink on hard board, and it will be the basis for the rest of the work. My illustrations are usually two or three times as large.

I prefer gouache and acrylic for airbrush artwork. I mix them until they're pretty opaque but still thin enough to get them through the airbrush.

For the actual airbrushing I only use one single instrument, a Thayer & Chandler with a single reservoir. This means that whenever I change colours I have to clean the airbrush and the reservoir thoroughly, of course. So I always have a big bucket of water next to my work table.

I always start with the lightest colours and work my way, step by step, down to black. Black is always the last colour I put on.

What I find extremely important is a clean studio. While I'm working on a picture – which usually takes two to three days – I always take the trouble to clean my entire work place thoroughly. This makes it a lot easier for me to keep my illustrations free dust and dirt.

And there is another positive side effect: it makes it a lot easier for me to concentrate fully on the necessary steps."

Top left: "Space Ship"
Format: 33 x 38 cm
Ground: illustration line board
Colours: Winsor & Newton gouache
Airbrush: Thayer & Chandler A
Commissioned by: Broderbund Inc.
1982 ©

Top right: "Galaga"
Format: 57.5 x 50.5 cm
Ground: illustration line board
Colours: Winsor & Newton gouache
Airbrush: Thayer & Chandler A
Commissioned by: Atari Inc. 1983 ©

Right: "Pole Position"
Format: 61.5 x 63 cm
Ground: illustration line board
Colours: Winsor & Newton gouache
Airbrush: Thayer & Chandler A
Commissioned by: Atari Inc. 1982 ©

Left: "Graphic Hand"
Intended use: advertising
Format: 82.5 x 66 cm
Ground: illustration line board
Colours: Winsor & Newton gouache
Airbrush: Thayer & Chandler A
Commissioned by: Letraset Inc.
1985 ©

Left: "Air Attack"
Format: 54 x 50.5 cm
Ground: illustration line board
Colours: Winsor & Newton gouache
Airbrush: Thayer & Chandler A
Commissioned by: Tronix 1982 ©

Below: "Space Kids"
Format: 54 x 76 cm
Ground: illustration line board
Colours: Winsor & Newton gouache
Airbrush: Thayer & Chandler A
Commissioned by: Digits Magazine 1985 ©

Right: "Jukebox"
Format: 82 x 66 cm
Ground: illustration line board
Colours: Winsor & Newton gouache
Airbrush: Thayer & Chandler A
Commissioned by: Oaksprings Inc. 1982 ©

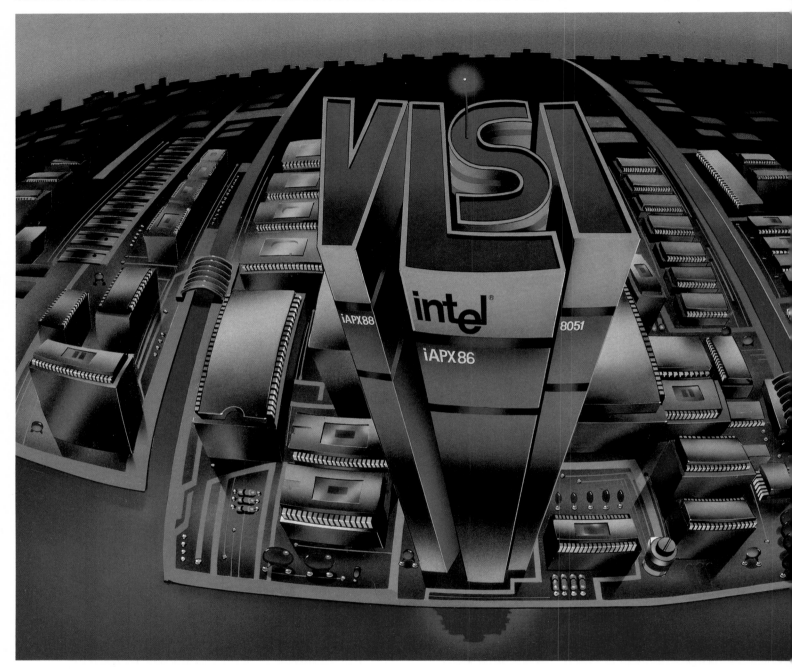

Above: "VLSI"
Format: 51 x 71 cm
Ground: illustration line board
Colours: Winsor & Newton gouache
Airbrush: Thayer & Chandler A
Commissioned by: Intel Inc. 1980 ©

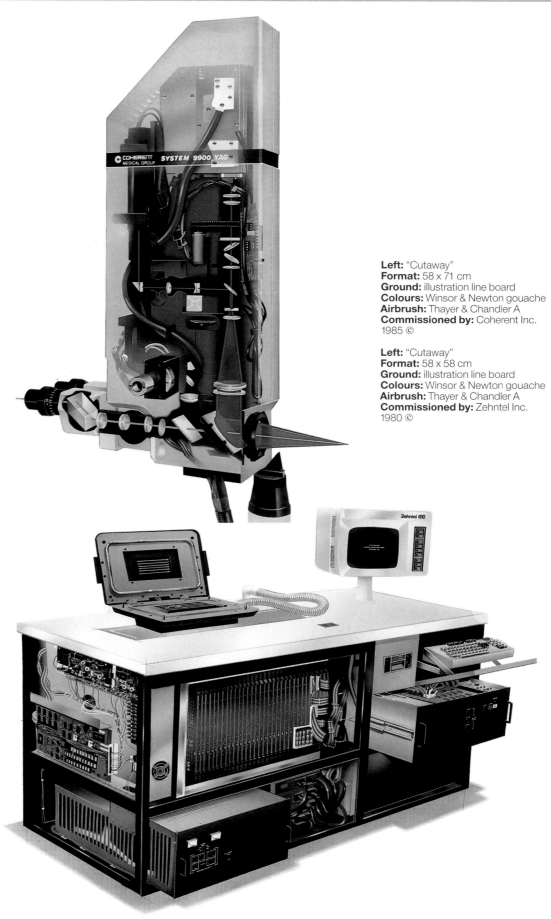

Left: "Cutaway"
Format: 58 x 71 cm
Ground: illustration line board
Colours: Winsor & Newton gouache
Airbrush: Thayer & Chandler A
Commissioned by: Coherent Inc.
1985 ©

Left: "Cutaway"
Format: 58 x 58 cm
Ground: illustration line board
Colours: Winsor & Newton gouache
Airbrush: Thayer & Chandler A
Commissioned by: Zehntel Inc.
1980 ©

PHIL EVANS is the youngest of the illustrators in this book. He is British but he decided to settle in Holland, where he feels very happy. Although he was born as late as 1962, he has already succeeded in making a name for himself, thanks to his extremely accurate technique, and is already working for international clients.

I would like to take this opportunity to express my special thanks to Phil for his willingness to sacrifice his Sunday for our interview.

METTE: You must have begun to draw at a very early age, Phil. When was that?

PHIL EVANS: At school, at the age of 14, I was extremely interested in everything to do with art. I used to make a lot of paintings with gouache and water-colour.

My interest in realism goes back to my time at school, too. I was only 16 when I first came across the airbrush. And as I was very ambitious I learnt very quickly.

What I enjoyed particularly was copying photos as realistically as possible with a paint-brush and an air-brush.

METTE: Did you continue to study art after school?

EVANS: Yes, I did a course in technical illustration at the Art College in Swansea. We started quite simply with black-and-white drawings, and later on we also made coloured illustrations.

METTE: And what did you do after college? You worked for an advertising agency, didn't you?

EVANS: That's right, I did. I started at a small studio. We used to work for British Steel, for instance, and I made small drawings and things like that. Usually illustrations.

Then I took on a few jobs for another agency in Newport. But it was about half an hour's car journey away, so that was rather stressful.

But only six months after I graduated I got another very important new contact. I was on my first holiday in Holland and I had taken along my portfolio with samples of my artwork. I showed them to a well-known agent here – and that was the beginning of it.

METTE: And so you stayed on in Holland.

EVANS: Yes, because I got my first job after only a very short period. I was asked to draw ten Mercedes lorries within four days.

METTE: What kind of models did you have?

EVANS: Polaroid photos. And a brochure. My greatest problem at that time was that I didn't have a projector for enlarging the photographs. So I had to work either freehand or I went into my girlfriend's college where they had an epidiascope.

METTE: Did you manage to keep the deadline?

EVANS: Of course I did! It was my first job, and I just had to finish it.

METTE: When was that?

EVENS: In February, 1983.

METTE: What about today? What kind of illustrations do you do most of the time? Mainly technology?

EVANS: Let me put it this way: about 30 percent are non-technical. There are all sorts of things. Also, I keep trying to perfect myself and so I practise a lot. For instance, structures with the airbrush, photographic realism and things like that.

METTE: I suppose you don't just use an airbrush, but you mix your techniques. Do you also use a paint-brush or coloured pencils?

EVANS: At first I used to use the paint-brush for covering up my shortcomings with the airbrush. Nowadays both brushes are on the same level, but I think the airbrush is more universal, more adaptable.

METTE: Which airbrushes do you use?

EVANS: The first one I had was a Paasche. I can't remember which model it was. The next one I bought was an Aerograph Super 63A from DeVilbiss.

I still use that one occasionally today, but about a year ago I decided to get a Paasche Turbo.

METTE: A first-class instrument – but how long did it take you to master it?

EVANS: I must admit that I didn't want to spoil any of my jobs. But then I was given a particularly difficult one by Bosch, and so I just started to use the Turbo.

Nothing went wrong on this job, but I would still say that it took me about six to nine months until I really felt safe.

Now I'm using almost nothing else. I haven't touched my other airbrushes since then. Though for large background areas I bought a DeVilbiss airbrush later.

METTE: So you've got over all your problems?

EVANS: I have, with the airbrush. But I haven't quite got used to the constant time pressure.

METTE: Do you ever find the time to do a few private, non-commercial jobs?

EVANS: Hardly ever, I'm afraid. Whenever I've finished a job, I'm so worn out that I can hardly do anything at all. So I go for walks or just have a rest. If at all possible, I just switch off completely.

METTE: What kind of paint do you use for your pictures?

EVANS: Usually transparent ink or glaze. But since I started using the Turbo I've also worked with gouache. That's partly because with gouache I can spray over a mistake occasionally, whereas I can't do that with dyes. And with gouache you can get a lot more intensity out of certain shades.

METTE: Finally, I'd like to ask you which ground you use for your pictures.

EVANS: Schoellershammer illustration line board.

METTE: The thick, laminated type?

EVANS: Yes. I always try to get my originals back and I think they are more resistant on thick hard board. And of course it looks better, so I just have slides made for the lithographic work.

METTE: Thank you very much – and I hope you continue to be successful in the future.

PHIL EVANS

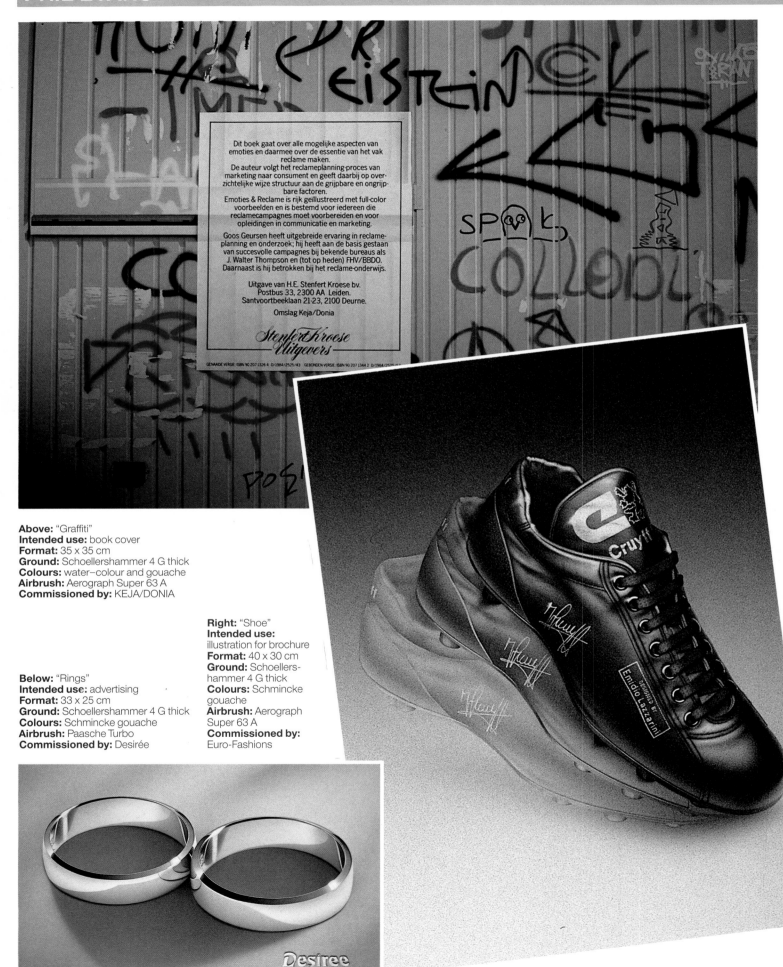

Above: "Graffiti"
Intended use: book cover
Format: 35 x 35 cm
Ground: Schoellershammer 4 G thick
Colours: water–colour and gouache
Airbrush: Aerograph Super 63 A
Commissioned by: KEJA/DONIA

Right: "Shoe"
Intended use:
illustration for brochure
Format: 40 x 30 cm
Ground: Schoellers-
hammer 4 G thick
Colours: Schmincke
gouache
Airbrush: Aerograph
Super 63 A
Commissioned by:
Euro-Fashions

Below: "Rings"
Intended use: advertising
Format: 33 x 25 cm
Ground: Schoellershammer 4 G thick
Colours: Schmincke gouache
Airbrush: Paasche Turbo
Commissioned by: Desirée

Dit boek gaat over alle mogelijke aspecten van emoties en daarmee over de essentie van het vak reclame maken.
De auteur volgt het reclameplanning-proces van marketing naar consument en geeft daarbij op overzichtelijke wijze structuur aan de grijpbare en ongrijpbare factoren.
Emoties & Reclame is rijk geïllustreerd met full-color voorbeelden en is bestemd voor iedereen die reclamecampagnes moet voorbereiden en voor opleidingen in communicatie en marketing.

Goos Geursen heeft uitgebreide ervaring in reclameplanning en onderzoek; hij heeft aan de basis gestaan van succesvolle campagnes bij bekende bureaus als J. Walter Thompson en (tot op heden) FHV/BBDO. Daarnaast is hij betrokken bij het reclame-onderwijs.

Uitgave van H.E. Stenfert Kroese bv.
Postbus 33, 2300 AA Leiden.
Santvoortbeeklaan 21-23, 2100 Deurne.

Omslag Keja/Donia

Stenfert Kroese Uitgevers

Left: "Logo 50"
Intended use: Logotype
Format: 30 x 30 cm
Ground: Schoellershammer 4 G thick
Colours: Schmincke gouache
Airbrush: Paasche Turbo
Commissioned by: Samen Sterk

Below: "Sherry"
Intended use: display
Format: 40 x 30 cm
Ground: Schoellershammer 4 G thick
Colours: Schmincke retouching paint
Airbrush: Aerograph Super 63 A
Commissioned by: Bobadilla

Left: "747"
Intended use: advertising
Format: 65 x 30 cm
Ground: Schoellershammer 4 G thick
Colours: Schmincke gouache
Airbrush: Paasche Turbo
Commissioned by: Japan Airlines

Above: "Tractor"
Intended use: technical illustration
Format: 30 x 20 cm
Ground: Schoellershammer 4 G thick
Colours: Schmincke gouache
Airbrush: Aerograph Super 63 A
Commissioned by: Cebeco

Right: "1619"
Intended use: technical illustration
Format: 45 x 33 cm
Ground: Schoellershammer 4 G thick
Colours: Schmincke gouache
Airbrush: Aerograph Super 63 A
Commissioned by: Mercedes

Following page: "Scissors"
Intended use: illustration for a book
on designing
Format: 40 x 30 cm
Ground: Schoellershammer 4 G thick
Colours: Schmincke gouache
Airbrush: Paasche Turbo
Commissioned by: Philips

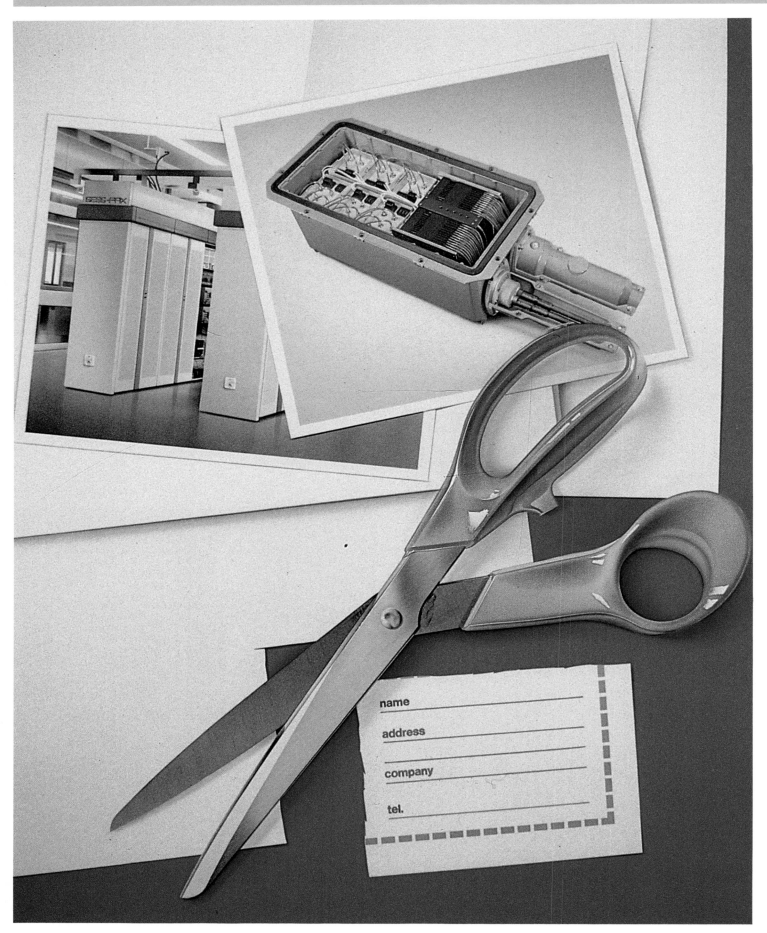

name _____

address _____

company _____

tel. _____

ROBERT EVANS lives and works in San Francisco, in the sunny state of California. He has been drawing things ever since he was a child, having started on his first cartoons at the tender age of nine.

So it followed logically that after school he joined an art academy. He graduated in 1976 and has been working as a freelance artist ever since.

He himself says that it took him about two years before he was totally independent. Until then he fought, like any other newcomer, for every client and every job. He has made a lot of illustrations for the computer industry, and you will

find a few examples on the following pages. When the growth rate of this industry was beginning to level off and there were no longer as many commissions as there had been, ROBERT EVANS had already become quite famous and was given work by other clients.

One of the areas where he specializes, for instance, is food, and a number of good pictures are included in this book. His main techniques are obviously those of commercial airbrush illustrations.

ROBERT EVANS paints or airbrushes all his artwork with opaque colours. When he started, he used Liquitex acrylics. Before putting the paint into the airbrush, he mixes and thins it down on a palette. In recent years he has also begun to experiment with other acrylic paints, such as Holbein, because of the relatively high degree of transparency of Liquitex. Occasionally, it would even shine through opaque white.

Whenever ROBERT EVANS does any work with the airbrush, he always wears a good face mask, even for the smallest piece of work. It is a safety precaution which he recommends to everyone who works with acrylics to prevent the pigment from damaging the lungs.

ROBERT EVANS uses three kinds of airbrushes: a Paasche VL-1 for large areas and broad outlines, an IWATA HP-B with a 0.2 mm nozzle for extremely delicate work, and an IWATA HP-SB for most other features. This is a model with changeable reservoirs, a feature he finds very useful for fast work.

For years he used to use carbon dioxide from a gas cylinder. It was cheap and there was very little condensation. It was only very recently that he started using a small compressor instead. He has got used to it by now and says that he would not want to do without it.

As a ground for his illustrations, ROBERT EVANS prefers several layers of laminated hard board if the work requires a stable surface, or a special kind of lightweight airbrush board, e.g. the one made by Carson's. For his masking work he always uses Zipatone film which has very low adhesive strength, and also thin, transparent acetate film. Apart from his illustrations with the airbrush, paintbrush and coloured pencil, he is also making increasing use of computer graphics. He has already tried out several hard and software systems and is hoping to do more of this kind of work in the future.

Top: Untitled
Intended use: advertising
Format: 38 x 30.5 cm
Ground: Crescent illustration line board
Colours: Liquitex and Holbein Opaque Colours
Airbrushes: Iwata HP-B and HP-SB, Paasche V1
Copyright: Robert Evans. All rights reserved.

Right: Untitled
Intended use: advertising
Format: 35.5 x 21 cm
Ground: Crescent illustration line board
Colours: Liquitex and Holbein Opaque Colours
Airbrushes: Iwata HP-B and HP-SB, Paasche V1
Copyright: Robert Evans. All rights reserved.

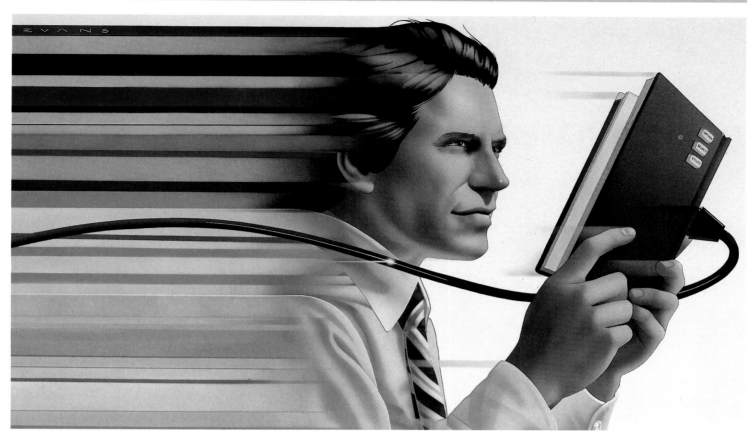

Left: Untitled
Intended use: advertising
Format: 61 x 45.5 cm
Ground: Crescent illustration line board
Colours: Liquitex and Holbein Opaque Colours
Airbrushes: Iwata HP-B and HP-SB, Paasche V1
Copyright: Robert Evans. All rights reserved.

Top: Untitled
Intended use: advertising
Format: 30.5 x 50.5 cm
Ground: Crescent illustration line board
Colours: Liquitex and Holbein Opaque Colours
Airbrushes: Iwata HP-B and HP-SB, Paasche V1
Copyright: Robert Evans. All rights reserved.

Right: Untitled
Intended use: advertising
Format: 61 x 48 cm
Ground: Crescent illustration line board
Colours: Liquitex and Holbein Opaque Colours
Airbrushes: Iwata HP-B and HP-SB, Paasche V1
Copyright: Robert Evans. All rights reserved.

ROBERT EVANS

Left: Untitled
Intended use: advertising
Format: 38 x 30.5 cm
Ground: Crescent illustration board
Colours: Liquitex and Holbein Opaque Colours
Airbrushes: Iwata HP-B and HP-SB, Paasche V1
Copyright: Robert Evans. All rights reserved.

Left below: Untitled
Intended use: advertising
Format: 42 x 32 cm
Ground: Crescent illustration line board
Colours: Liquitex and Holbein Opaque Colours
Airbrushes: Iwata HP-B and HP-SB, Paasche V1
Copyright: Robert Evans. All rights reserved.

Top right: Untitled
Intended use: advertising
Format: 43 x 33 cm
Ground: Crescent illustration line board
Colours: Liquitex and Holbein Opaque Colours
Airbrushes: Iwata HP-B and HP-SB, Paasche V1
Copyright: Robert Evans. All rights reserved.

Left: Untitled
Intended use: advertising
Format: 38 x 30.5 cm
Ground: Crescent illustration line board
Colours: Liquitex and Holbein Opaque Colours
Airbrushes: Iwata HP-B and HP-SB, Paasche V1
Copyright: Robert Evans. All rights reserved.

Below: Untitled
Intended use: advertising
Format: 45.5 x 45.5 cm
Ground: Crescent illustration line board
Colours: Liquitex and Holbein Opaque Colours
Airbrushes: Iwata HP-B and HP-SB, Paasche V1
Copyright: Robert Evans. All rights reserved.

Left: Untitled
Intended use: advertising
Format: 43 x 45.5 cm
Ground: Crescent illustration line board
Colours: Liquitex and Holbein Opaque Colours
Airbrushes: Iwata HP-B and HP-SB, Paasche V1
Copyright: Robert Evans. All rights reserved.

Below: Untitled
Intended use: advertising
Format: 33 x 38 cm
Ground: Crescent illustration line board
Colours: Liquitex and Holbein Opaque Colours
Airbrushes: Iwata HP-B and HP-SB, Paasche V1
Copyright: Robert Evans. All rights reserved.

METTE: Would you mind telling our readers how old you are, Rick?

GOODALE: Not at all. I'm 42.

METTE: And you were born in Britain?

GOODALE: Yes, in Wales. On 26th September, 1943.

METTE: How did you first come across the airbrush?

GOODALE: When I left school, unlike many other illustrators, I didn't know anything about the airbrush at all.

Then I got a job working for an uncle of mine who had a large printer's workshop in London. I started work at his studio. Just odd jobs, really, but I could watch other illustrators and designers at work. I did this for about four years. At that time I learnt the basic techniques, such as making technical drawings.

Then I changed over to the Sunday Times where I met Alan Aldridge. He had already had some experience with the airbrush and was quite a well-known illustrator. We made friends and joined Penguin Books together, that's where Alan was my art director.

METTE: When was that?

GOODALE: In the sixties. Our work always followed the same pattern: Alan made the illustrations with the contours and I coloured them in with the airbrush.

Then, in the late sixties, Alan founded "Ink Studios". This was probably the centre for illustrators in London at the time. We used to work for a number of very wellknown clients, such as the Rolling Stones and the Beatles.

We worked together for about four years until, with a colleague, I started the first studio of my own, the "Drawing Room". We were able to take over some of our old clients because Alan Aldridge wanted to work on some new projects. So we had a fair amount of work to do.

We carried on working very successfully for two or three years. Then I felt like travelling. I packed my bags and moved to Amsterdam, the place which I thought would be most suitable for my way to life.

METTE: And how long did you stay in Amsterdam?

GOODALE: For about two years. It was the time of the hippies in Amsterdam. Good fun and a nice change. It was must have been around 1972 or 73.

And then I met Ann, my wife, who is Swedish. So I moved to Sweden and worked there for a while. Then we went back to London for the next few years.

In fact, I spent a good five years as a freelance artist providing all the agencies which I had got to know in previous years with illustrations. Those were already international jobs.

METTE: Did you have any firm agents at the time?

GOODALE: Yes, I had brought along some good contacts from abroad. There was an agent in Amsterdam, one in Belgium and another in Paris.

The French market seems to be a very good one anyway. As well as commissions which I got through my Paris agent, I also managed to get a lot of work through my own advertising.

But to come back to my love of travelling. I had found a marvellous partner in my wife, because after about five years of London we had had enough of it again and decided to go to Australia for a change.

It really was just as simple as I'm telling you now. We wanted to go to Australia so we bought our tickets and flew off, which took us only a couple of days. And we stayed there for two years.

Then we moved to Los Angeles. Because of the Olympics. We managed to stay there for a year and a half. And we've been back in London for about a year now.

What really made the most lasting impression on us in all our travelling was the large number of people we met. Both privately and business-wise. If you want to, you really do meet a lot of people.

METTE: And what does it feel like to be at home after such a long time abroad?

GOODALE: We've settled in again. I've got into touch again with all my old contacts and told them that I'm back.

Which reminds me – one of my greatest problems as an illustrator is that people hardly ever remember my good works. I made first-class illustrations for some of my clients for years, but if one of them wasn't quite so good, they still remember it today.

I've learnt in recent years that you can't afford to produce inferior quality even once. In spite of all the time pressure which the commercial illustrator has to face!

In fact, it's because of the time pressure that you can't work on one particular picture until you're really happy with it. I've often found that frustrating. That's why I'm not an artist but a commercial artist. I suppose it's something you just have to live with.

METTE: Do you never actually feel that you'd like to work just for yourself? That would be a lot more satisfying, wouldn't it?

GOODALE: No, not while I'm earning my living with illustrations. Later perhaps. But today, when I've got a little bit of free time, I'd rather go for a walk or have a glass of beer. That's how I relax from my stressful job.

METTE: How long do you reckon you'll be able to carry on if it means so much stress for you?

GOODALE: No idea. But I'm always looking for new things. Maybe something will come up one day. I have been finding anyway that the trend towards illustrations is no longer particularly strong in the agencies.

METTE: That's interesting. How come?

GOODALE: I suppose it's because those who are responsible in the various agencies, i.e. the art directors, prefer to have 60 percent of the pictures in the form of photographs rather than in illustrations.

If they employ an illustrator, they might see him three times within two weeks. When he is given the job, after the first layout and when the picture is handed in. But if you can be in a photo studio with a lot of pretty girls and a cup of coffee or a glass of wine, that's a lot more pleasant, isn't it?

METTE: It is indeed. Illustrators ought to have a lot more contact with other people – and each other, too.

GOODALE: That's a point I find particularly important. Every now and then I try to find time to meet with as many people as possible. And it's not bad for business, either. To my mind, it's just as much part of a profess-ional attitude as doing good work.

METTE: I do hope you'll continue to be successful.

Above: Untitled
Format: 48 x 74 cm
Ground: CS10 Line Board
Colours: Pelikan drawing ink
Airbrushes: DeVilbiss Super 63 A and Super 63 E
Commissioned by: Autoart Canada

Below: Untitled
Intended use: technical illustration
Format: 60 x 80 cm
Ground: Schoellershammer hard board
Colours: Pelikan drawing ink and gouache
Airbrushes: DeVilbiss Super 63 A and Super 63 E
Commissioned by: Volvo, Australia

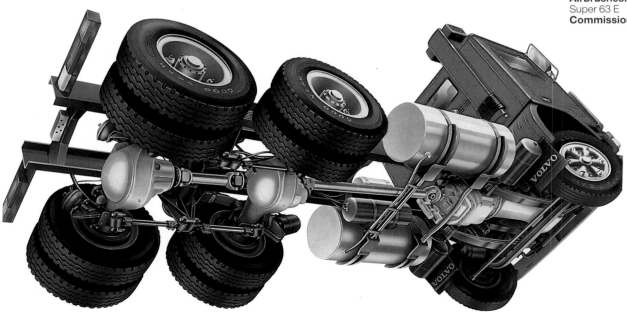

Above: Untitled
Format: 70 x 50 cm
Ground: Crescent illustration line
board
Colours: India ink, acrylic and
gouache
Airbrushes: DeVilbiss Super 63 A and
Super 63 E
Commissioned by: CBS, U.S.A.

Right: Untitled
Format: 36 x 25 cm
Ground: Schoellershammer hard board
Colours: Pelikan drawing ink
Airbrushes: DeVilbiss Super 63 A and Super 63 E
Commissioned by: Heinz, Sweden

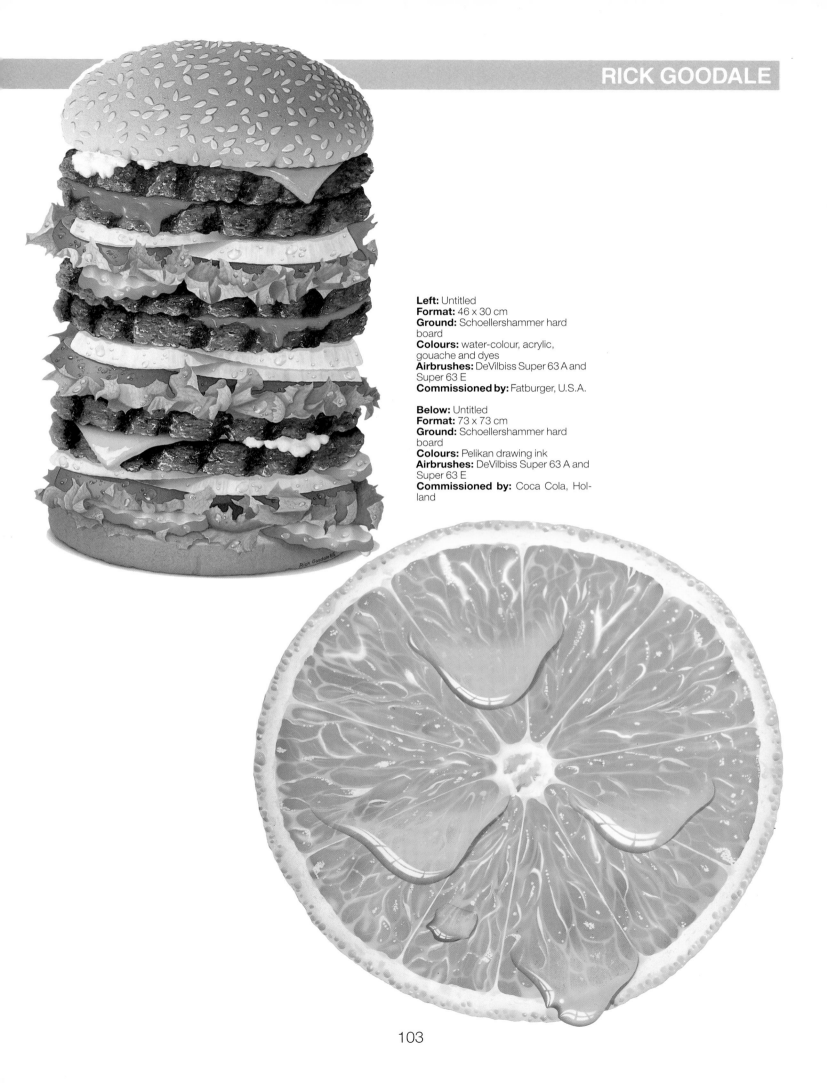

Left: Untitled
Format: 46 x 30 cm
Ground: Schoellershammer hard board
Colours: water-colour, acrylic, gouache and dyes
Airbrushes: DeVilbiss Super 63 A and Super 63 E
Commissioned by: Fatburger, U.S.A.

Below: Untitled
Format: 73 x 73 cm
Ground: Schoellershammer hard board
Colours: Pelikan drawing ink
Airbrushes: DeVilbiss Super 63 A and Super 63 E
Commissioned by: Coca Cola, Holland

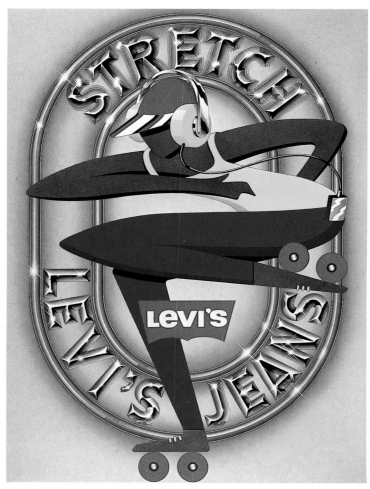

Top left: "My Own Car"
Intended use: magazine illustration
Format: 40 x 70 cm
Ground: CS 10 line board
Colours: Pelikan drawing ink
Airbrushes: DeVilbiss Super 63 A and
Super 63 E
Commissioned by: Car Magazine,
U.K.

Facing page, bottom left: "Colour
Cup"
Intended use: artist's signet
Format: 80 x 50 cm
Ground: Schoellershammer hard
board
Colours: Pelikan drawing ink and
gouache
Airbrushes: DeVilbiss Super 63 A and
Super 63 E

Facing page, bottom right: Untitled
Intended use: logotype
Format: 76 x 51 cm
Ground: illustration line board
Colours: Pelikan drawing ink
Airbrushes: DeVilbiss Super 63 A and
Super 63 E
Commissioned by: Levi's, U.K.

Right: Untitled
Format: 80 x 60 cm
Ground: CS 10 line board
Colours: acrylic and dyes
Airbrushes: DeVilbiss Super 63 A and
Super 63 E
Commissioned by: Pepsi Cola,
Norway

TE OSTERWALDER is now living and working in exactly the same place which served as her starting point for conquering the world of illustrations: in Hamburg. My first impression of her studio was that of a vast number of pictures. Every single wall was covered from top to bottom with sketches, layouts and finished illustrations.

Her style could be described as a kind of fantastic realism. There were mainly medical subjects: visual aids that could be understood without too much medical knowledge and which had been printed in various popularized scientific books or magazines. Nearly every renowned magazine has made use of her illustrations at some stage.

UTE OSTERWALDER is quite well-known as an illustrator today. Interestingly, though, she came to it as a matter of mere chance.

UTE OSTERWALDER: That's a funny story. When I had finished school, I didn't really know what I was going to do. But a friend of mine had an idea. She was going to join the Hamburg Fashion School.

As she was rather nervous about the entrance exam, I agreed to give her some moral support and to take the exam as well. I actually passed it and was admitted to the college.

I got a bit worried when, after my first year, I was told by my teachers that I wasn't gifted enough at drawing. So I changed courses, i.e. to calligraphy and photography. This meant that drawing and illustrating was going to be 'out' for the next few years.

METTE: But somehow you managed to get into it again. How did that happen?

OSTERWALDER: My husband, who was also an illustrator, used to keep saying that my work was really nice. And so I gradually began to take it up again.

It all started properly with medical illustrations for a popular scientific publication. In fact, popularized scientific illustrations have constantly been present through the whole of my career. It's because I enjoy learning and understanding things.

At first we used to work for the German magazine TWEN, and that was how the advertising agencies got hold of us: Margarethe Hubauer was in fact very helpful as an agent.

METTE: What kind of jobs do you get most of the time?

OSTERWALDER: It varies a lot these days. Of course I prefer the ones that pay best, and they're usually advertisements. But I don't want this to get out of hand, so now and again I accept jobs from newspapers and magazines.

METTE: Are there any techniques which you're particularly fond of in your work?

OSTERWALDER: Yes, I prefer working with a paintbrush or a pen. And of course with the airbrush. I'm sure I do about half my work with the airbrush. Sometimes it's only backgrounds and large areas, but sometimes also finer contours and details.

METTE: Which airbrushes do you actually use?

OSTERWALDER: I started with those gigantic ones which are also used for spraying cars. There were practical reasons for that. I used to prefer acrylic at the time, and I didn't find the smaller airbrushes very suitable for that. I have of course used glaze in the past, but it meant that I wasn't even allowed to sneeze, and after every single little corner I had to reckon on two or three hours of retouching.

My favourite airbrush is made by a firm here in Hamburg, called Harder & Steenbeck. It's not a very well-known one, but I've really got used to it by now. It's very hard-wearing, extremely easy to clean, and even if you drop it on the floor once in a while, it doesn't immediately give up the ghost. I also use Olympos airbrushes in various sizes, and of course a normal-size EFBE.

METTE: I noticed that you use a compressor to supply the air for your airbrushes. Have you always used one, or was there a time when you used to have carbon dioxide or something like that?

OSTERWALDER: We bought the compressor in Zurich, and I've been working with it right from the beginning.

METTE: And it's always been photographic realism?

OSTERWALDER: "Photographic realism" isn't really the right word. Even my clients, the agencies tend to refer to my work as that "peculiar kind of naturalism". That's what my work is always called.

METTE: How would you refer to it?

OSTERWALDER: Well, it is a kind of realism of course, but a lot more graphic, more reduced, more indirect.

METTE: Earlier on you mentioned that you used to prefer acrylics as your favourite paint. Is that still true?

OSTERWALDER: No, I decided to get my India ink out again because when I use acrylics, my pictures tend to come out rather too grey quite frequently. If you often have to go over the same area again and again, which is what I do, then you almost get a grey haze. Gouache is quite good for avoiding this, too.

METTE: Which ground do you use most of the time?

OSTERWALDER: That really depends on the kind of work I'm doing. At the moment I'm going through a phase where I use a lot of illustration line board. But there was a time when I preferred canvas, to make the pictures look more lively.

METTE: Could you comment on the formats you use?

OSTERWALDER: They tend to be on the large side. That's how I started and I've never changed. When I first saw other people's airbrush artwork, I used to ask myself how they managed to do it so perfectly.

My solution – and I think most people do the same – was to use large formats which could be reduced in size quite a lot afterwards.

METTE: Just one final, general question: would you be able to make illustrations without the airbrush at all?

OSTERWALDER: Hardly. There are always a number of jobs that can really only be tackled with the airbrush. At least, when it comes to advertising and the client wants his product to be recognized in a certain way.

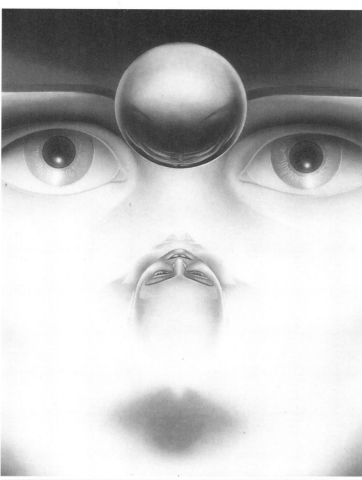

Left: "Hypnosis"
Intended use: magazine illustration
Format: 50 x 45 cm
Ground: hard board
Colours: acrylic
Airbrush: Ultra F 15
Commissioned by: Swiss family

Below: "A New Storm in the Sky"
Intended use: magazine illustration
Format: 70 x 50 cm
Ground: hard board
Colours: India ink
Airbrush: Ultra F 15
Commissioned by: Playboy

Following page, top: Untitled
Intended use: front page for
"Ullstein's Gourmet Journal"
Format: 50 x 70 cm
Ground: canvas
Colours: acrylic
Airbrush: Ultra F 15
Commissioned by: Ullstein's
Gourmet Journal

First picture, below: Untitled
Intended use: front page for "Ullstein's Gourmet Journal"
Format: 50 x 70 cm
Ground: canvas
Colours: acrylic
Airbrush: Ultra F 15
Commissioned by: Ullstein's Gourmet Journal

Second picture, below: Untitled
Intended use: front page for "Ullstein's Gourmet Journal"
Format: 50 x 70 cm
Ground: canvas
Colours: acrylic
Airbrush: Ultra F 15
Commissioned by: Ullstein's Gourmet Journal

Bottom right: "Herbs in the Woods, Fields and Meadows"
Intended use: magazine cover
Format: 50 x 70 cm
Ground: canvas
Colours: acrylic
Airbrush: Ultra F 15
Commissioned by: Zeit magazine

Top left: "Fresh on the Table"
Intended use: magazine illustration
Format: 50 x 70 cm
Ground: canvas
Colours: acrylic
Airbrush: Ultra F 15
Commissioned by: Playboy

Top right: Untitled
Intended use: "Ullstein's Gourmet Journal"
Format: 50 x 70 cm
Ground: canvas
Colours: acrylic
Airbrush: Ultra F 15
Commissioned by: Ullstein's Gourmet Journal

Left: Untitled
Intended use: advertising
Format: 100 x 70 cm
Ground: hard board
Colours: India ink
Airbrush: Ultra F 15
Commissioned by: Wunder Werbe-beratung GmbH

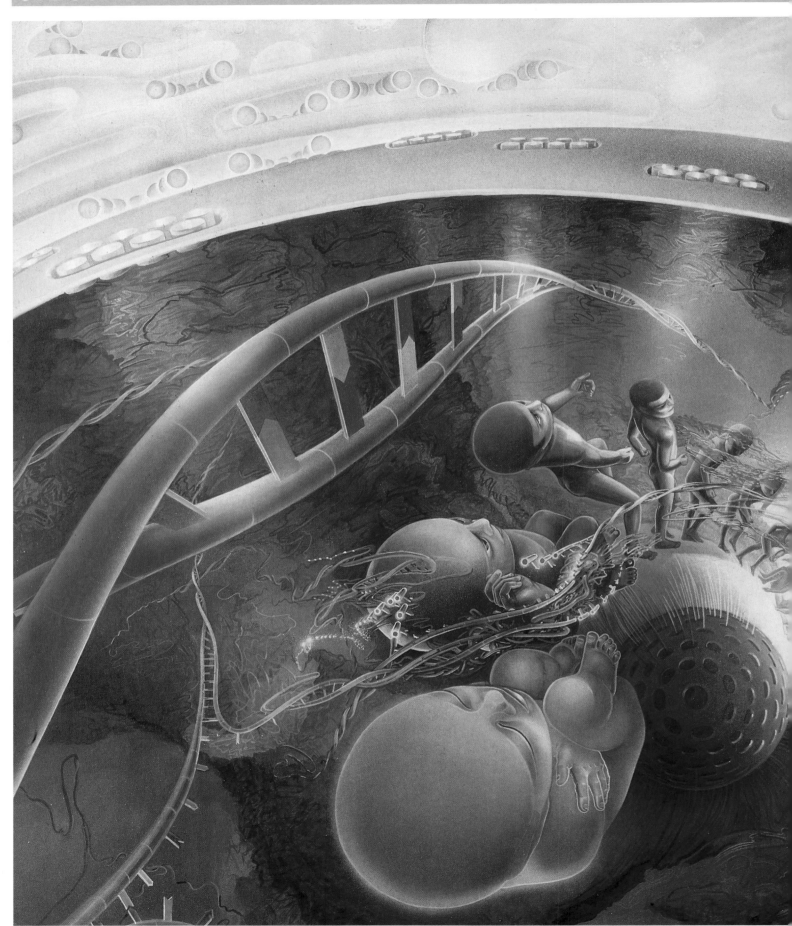

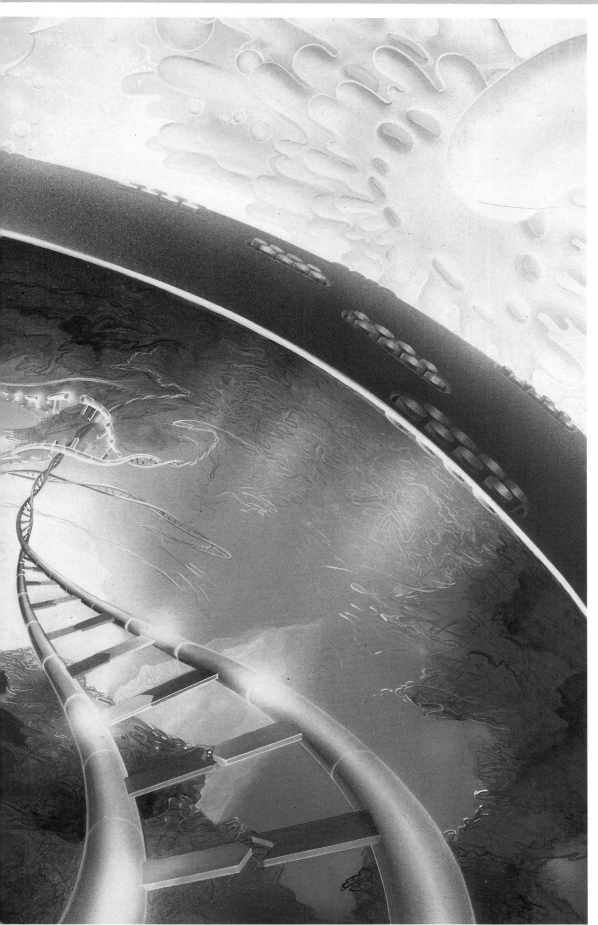

Left: "Genetic Research"
Intended use: magazine illustration
Format: 100 x 70 cm
Ground: canvas
Colours: acrylic
Airbrushes: Ultra F 15 and Olympos 100 B
Commissioned by: Stern magazine

Right: "Smoker's Heart"
Intended use: advertising
Format: 70 x 60 cm
Ground: canvas
Colours: acrylic
Airbrush: Ultra F 15
Commissioned by: Luders, Cologne
(advertising agency)

Bottom left: "In the Jungle of
Emotions"
Intended use: magazine cover
Format: 70 x 50 cm
Ground: canvas
Colours: acrylic
Airbrush: Ultra F 15
Commissioned by: Zeit magazine

Bottom right: "In the Jungle of
Emotions"
Intended use: magazine illustration
Format: 70 x 50 cm
Ground: canvas
Colours: acrylic
Airbrush: Ultra F 15
Commissioned by: Zeit magazine

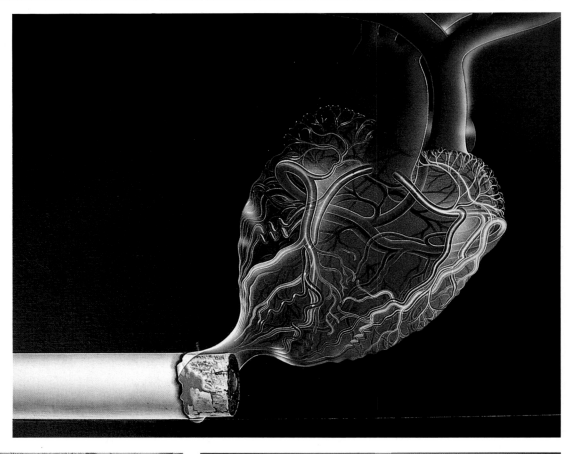

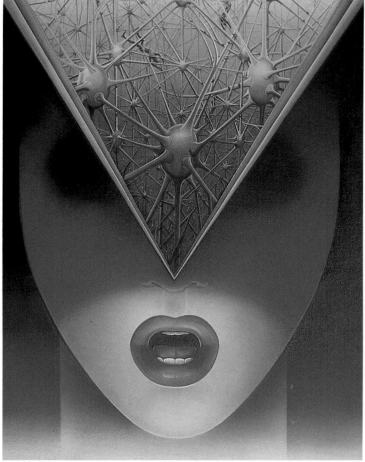

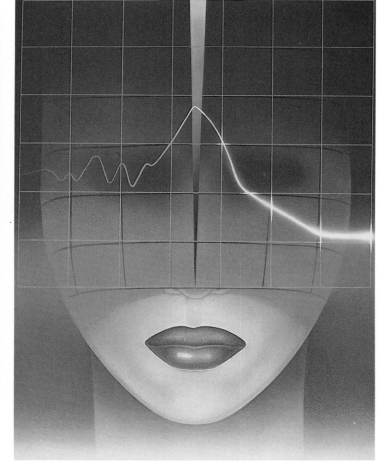

H EINZ RÖHRIG, born in 1949, is an illustrator and graphic designer. He lives and works in Frankfurt and most of his clients are agencies.

METTE: Could you tell our readers something about yourself and your work? How did your career as an illustrator begin?

RÖHRIG: I left school at the age of 16 and joined a private art college called Westend Schule here in Frankfurt. Then I changed to a state college in Offenbach, where my three years in Frankfurt were credited. I finished my course in Offenbach with a diploma in 1974.

Basically, the training consisted of two components. There was a practical side to it and one that put the emphasis on a purely theoretical kind of education.

METTE: Where did you put the emphasis, and what was it like?

RÖHRIG: The practical part of my course was no doubt the more important one for my development as an illustrator. There's one example that springs to mind. We had a lecturer at the private college who made us draw animals quite a lot. And oddly enough, he always used to notice immediately when we had got our subjects from the zoo and when we had got them from the museum. At the beginning it was rather difficult to draw animals which kept moving, but after six months I managed.

Experiences like this were incredibly important during my training, I think.

METTE: What didn't you like about the theory?

RÖHRIG: I wouldn't put it quite so bluntly. I didn't really dislike anything. All I know is that, with hindsight, I got more out of the practical training than I did from the theoretical.

As soon as I had my diploma and the right letters after my name, I was let loose, so to speak, and I could start working. My portfolio was perfectly all right, but I always had a feeling that they were laughing their heads off at the agencies when they saw someone like me coming along with his impressive title.

This is still the same. There are people who've been to college and who've had a lot of academic training, but they're incapable of making a simple drawing.

Mind you, I've got nothing against theory in principle. But the practical side shouldn't be neglected, either.

METTE: There's no doubt that you're very skilful, so if you didn't acquire your skills at college, where did you learn them?

RÖHRIG: Simply by taking on odd vacation jobs. I was lucky at the time and managed to get a kind of work-experience job at a publishing company. And then again and again during college vacations for next two years. In the production department.

That was where I learnt, for instance, how to use a slide rule. Nobody ever taught me that at college.

Even nowadays students don't get the best kind of training in that respect. The jobs I get include not only pure illustrations but also brochures, story boards, posters and things like that. Occasionally I also employ a student, but unfortunately their practical knowledge does tend to be rather appaling.

METTE: How could college training be improved then?

RÖHRIG: I would compare it with music: improvising, like in jazz, is really only possible if you know your craft really well, right from the beginning.

To put it professionally: what's the use of a colleague if I can have learned discussions with him, but he can't even draw?

METTE: What form do you think training ought to take, and how do you think it should change in the future?

RÖHRIG: Well, first of all, we need a consensus on what our profession is all about. So far nobody really seems to know what a graphic designer is and what he does. And once there is a general framework, then young people can get more guidance and better training. The aim can then be found quite easily.

METTE: I'd like to come back to your own life. What did you do after college?

RÖHRIG: I was extremely lucky. A friend of my father's had a small graphic design studio, and I was allowed to become his partner straight away. So I was self-employed at the very beginning.

METTE: Did you like it? Or did you find it difficult to get used to it?

RÖHRIG: My partner was a real graphic designer of the old calibre. He only ever worked for clients directly. After a while, I wasn't satisfied with that of course, and so I tried to get some closer contacts with the agencies. I thought it was too dangerous to drift into just one particular direction.

My desire to go into the big wide world of advertising was a bit suspect to my partner at the time. So we separated after four years, and I continued to work as a freelance artist, i.e. independently.

METTE: What kind of commissions did you get?

RÖHRIG: A lot of layout work at first and occasionally the odd drawing. But most of the time I worked with a felt pen.

METTE: You acquired your airbrush skills and knowledge gradually over the years, as a sideline, didn't you?

RÖHRIG: It came quite automatically. The agencies thought very highly of me as an illustrator and so I was given the appropriate jobs.

For example, when I was asked to produce a photographically accurate picture of a box that didn't actually exist at that stage, I just had to illustrate it. And the airbrush was the idea tool to achieve such an effect. So I bought one and started to work with it. I just had to, you see.

METTE: Do you use pigments or water-based paints?

RÖHRIG: I use Schmincke retouching paint for most of my illustrations. This is a very fine pigment which comes in tubes, and I thin it down to a sprayable consistency. Occasionally I also use glaze.

METTE: You need a lot of drafts for your technical illustrations. Do you make them yourself?

RÖHRIG: That's right, I do. Usually together with a competent adviser of my client, such as the art director of the agency. It's extremely hard work.

Take the chassis of the lorry. I did have a photograph of it, but there just wasn't enough light in it, and it was such a mess that a draft was necessary. So that's what I did.

METTE: Which ground do you use for your work?

RÖHRIG: Illustration line board. Sometimes with a smooth surface, sometimes rough, depending on the kind of structures I want to achieve.

Most agencies nowadays demand illustrations that will fit round the scanner. So I use 250-gram hard board, which can be wrapped round the scanner quite easily.

I have actually seen lithographers who tried to detach the top layer of the thick laminated hard board. In fact quite a lot of originals have been destroyed in this way.

METTE: Are there any particular formats which you prefer?

RÖHRIG: I wouldn't say 'prefer'. They're usually 50 x 70 cm. There's a simple practical reason: you can be more accurate with details.

METTE: Now that we know which materials you prefer to work with, can you just tell us which airbrushes you use?

RÖHRIG: I started with an EFBE, which is a single-action one, and I've been using it ever since. I've got so much used to it that I shall continue to use it in the future.

After a while I also acquired an AEROGRAPH Super 63, but I had quite a few problems getting used to the double-action lever. I'm all right now, though.

Left: Untitled
Intended use: illustration for competition
Format: 45 x 60 cm
Ground: illustration line board
Colours: gouache
Airbrush: EFBE A1
Commissioned by: Pfauntsch & Partners
Client: Wrangler

Below: Untitled
Intended use: window sticker
Format: 50 x 50 cm
Ground: illustration line board
Colours: gouache
Airbrush: EFBE A1
Commissioned by: Pfauntsch & Partners
Client: Wrangler

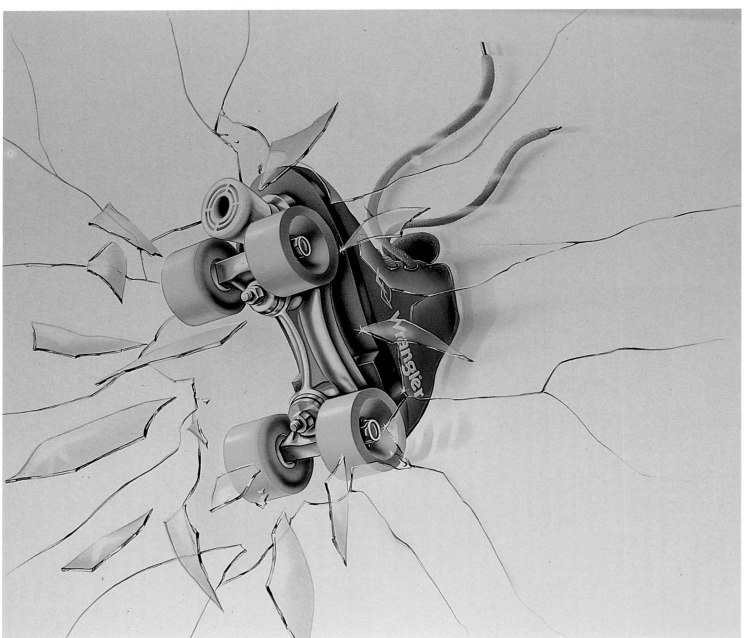

Left: Motor-Car Chassis
Intended use: technical illustration
Format: 70 x 100 cm
Ground: illustration line board
Colours: gouache
Airbrush: EFBE A1
Commissioned by: Ted Bates.
Client: Honda

Below: Untitled
Intended use: advertising
Format: 80 x 90 cm
Ground: illustration line board
Colours: gouache
Airbrush: EFBE A1
Commissioned by: Pfauntsch & Partners
Client: Danone

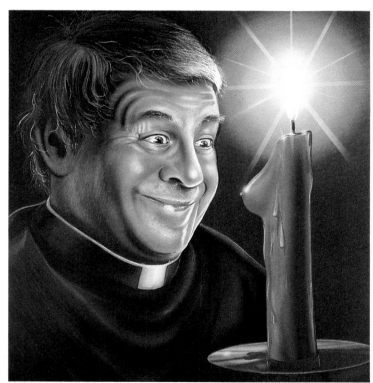

Above: Untitled
Format: 36 x 40 cm
Ground: illustration line board
Colours: gouache
Airbrush: EFBE A1

Left: Untitled
Intended use: advertising
Format: 60 x 70 cm
Ground: illustration line board
Colours: gouache
Airbrush: EFBE A1
Commissioned by: Schnell & Partners
Client: Bolte

HEINZ RÖHRIG

Right: Untitled
Intended use: self-promotion
Format: 50 x 60 cm
Ground: illustration line board
Colours: gouache and coloured pencil
Airbrush: EFBE A1

122

Left: Untitled
Format: 29 x 45 cm
Ground: illustration line board
Colours: gouache, stipple technique
Airbrush: EFBE A1

Below: Untitled
Unpublished
Format: 21 x 29 cm
Ground: illustration line board
Colours: gouache
Airbrush: EFBE A1

PETER RÖSELER is unique in that he did not decide to follow his interest in illustrating until relatively late. He was born in Magdeburg, East Germany, in 1934, and is married with two children.

Having inherited his creative talent from his father, he decided to opt for a secure job at first and began to train as a process designer, then he moved to West Germany in 1949, where he worked for a reprographic studio. After a while he began to take evening classes and, following the advice of his teacher, became a fulltime student at a college called Folkwangschule in Essen.

Having a family to provide for, he took the safe path into various advertising institutions. First he worked for a commercial art studio, then an advertising agency and finally he became the head of an advertising department in industry.

About three years ago PETER RÖSELER became fed up with the stress and went independent, now working as a freelance artist.

METTE: When did you come across the airbrush for the first time?

PETER RÖSELER: Years ago, in 1963, when I was on work-experience at a reprographic studio. It gave me the opportunity to watch a real, properly trained retoucher at work. It fascinated me so much that I decided to learn that as well.

METTE: Had you always wanted to take up retouching, from the very beginning?

RÖSELER: No, I never wanted to do that. At this studio they were looking for someone who could do everything, ranging from illustrations to retouching. So I read everything I could lay my hands on, tried generally to find out as much as I could – and took the plunge. And in fact it worked quite well at first. I retouched everthing I could get hold of, and after a very short time I even managed some very complicated machineretouching. That was the time when I was laying the foundations of my present skills. Because of that and also thanks to a colleague, I managed to acquire quite a few tricks and skills.

METTE: You said you found out a lot through reading. Had anything been written about retouching or the airbrush at that time?

RÖSELER: Yes. I brought a book over from East Germany, published in Leipzig, in fact as early as 1923. There was a lot about airbrush technique in it.

METTE: I'd like to come back to your first few years at the reprographics studio. Do you still remember which airbrush you used when you first tried your hand at airbrushing?

RÖSELER: It was a GRAFO with a 0.15 mm nozzle.

METTE: I know that you still use the GRAFO today. When did you first buy your own airbrush?

RÖSELER: At about that time, around 1965. I think I got it through a company called Klimsch. If I remember correctly, it cost me about 220 German marks (then £24).

METTE: What about the air-supply system? What sort of equipment did you have?

RÖSELER: Gas-cylinders. In fact, I used to have them until about eighteen months ago. Then I changed over to compressors and bought a small 30-litre compressor from LETRASET.

The disadvantage about the cylinder was that there came a point when it was almost empty but you couldn't really work out from the pressure meter how long exactly it was going to last.

And so again and again I used to run out of air whenever I had to do a quick job over the weekend. It got me into quite a lot of difficulties. It was something I simply didn't want to risk when I went independent.

METTE: And did you work with the airbrush all those years?

RÖSELER: No, I didn't. While I was an advertising manager in industry, I couldn't work with it for about ten years. I just didn't have the time! And I couldn't really concentrate on it, either.

Then after all those years in management I reached the point where I felt I wanted to be creative again, and so I got my old airbrush out. At first I could only work at weekends, and for a while I just illustrated for my own enjoyment.

METTE: How did you actually acquire your knowledge of the airbrush technique?

RÖSELER: When I was still in Magdeburg, I trained as a process engraver. Then I moved to West Germany and worked in a lithographic studio. And as I had always been interested in painting and drawing, I started going to evening classes at the Folkwangschule.

My teacher, Jo Pieper, who was quite a well-known painter, suggested that I should study full-time. But I needed money, so I continued to work as a lithographer in the evenings and studied during the day. Although I had a small grant, it didn't actually strech very far.

METTE: Were you taught about the airbrush technique at college in those days?

RÖSELER: Oh no, we weren't. Although the airbrush was mentioned, it was largely ignored in practice.

METTE: That doesn't seem to have changed much in Germany.

RÖSELER: Well, this isn't England or America. I read of a famous German illustrator the other day who said that he didn't like working with the airbrush at all. He finds the results too cold and smooth. And I have in fact noticed that airbrush artists do tend to paint human beings as if they were rubber dolls or as if they were wearing inflated diving suits.

That's why I don't just use the airbrush for my illustrations, but I try to vary the techniques.

METTE: This is getting interesting now. Could you tell us something about your own experiences?

RÖSELER: Certainly. For instance, even with small areas, I avoid stencils that cause sharp edges. Instead, I use my own finger or a nail to cover portions of a picture. If you use a firmly fixed stencil you're bound to get contours that are very harsh. Or, when I use a French curve, I put it down at a slight angle. I still get the desired shape, but it's a lot softer.

Also, to get lighter areas and highlights, I do a lot of wiping. Sometimes with a paintbrush and sometimes with a piece of cotton wool.

METTE: Do you ever use a rubber for highlights?

RÖSELER: Yes, of course, a hard one.

METTE: What kind of paint do you prefer?

RÖSELER: Gouache. I nearly always use opaque colours – very occasionally transparent ones. This is probably because I used to do a lot of retouching when I first started. With these colours I can put anything into practice that I can imagine. There are hardly any problems.

METTE: Do you mix your colours in advance or not until you actually need them?

RÖSELER: I mix them on palettes and then just leave them. It doesn't matter if the paint dries up, I can always make it liquid again. I think that's very practical. In fact, I don't go back to it again until a palette has been lying around for a while and gathered dust and various other things.

METTE: I suppose you learnt all this gradually through experience?

RÖSELER: I did. But I think there are other things which should be practised, not just the mixing of colours. I have noticed again and again that people buy an ex-pensive piece of equipment, such as an airbrush, and then think the rest will just come automatically.
Well, it won't. The most important basis for good illustrations is a well-trained eye and a well-trained hand. Rather than relying on technique, one should train drawing and composition a lot more.

METTE: How did you choose your subjects, and where did you get your models from?

RÖSELER: To be honest, I enjoy working from photographs. It doesn't matter where the photo comes from. I love changing things and taking them out of their original contexts.

Sometimes I've got something definite in mind and I start looking for it. But it also happens that I approach a topic rather more randomly, i.e. by getting a general idea of a topic area, say, cars.

In fact, this is also the point at which I start paying attention to the finer points of style, such as whether the individual elements fit together or not.

METTE: Do you have a subject archive?

RÖSELER: Well, as time goes by, quite a lot of material accumulates, of course. I collect everything I find interesting.

METTE: How do you start an illustration?

RÖSELER: First of all, I make several broad sketches to fit the various elements of a picture together. This is mainly a matter of composition and proportion. After these scribbles I work out the basic shapes.

Once these basic areas have been fixed, I go over the whole lot again. And occasionally I may have to balance out the dark areas, i.e. the shadows.

I always try to produce photographic realism without harshness. So I use the paint-brush quite a lot, too, and try to aim at the right mixing technique.

METTE: How do you, for instance, solve the problem of painting hair?

RÖSELER: I start off by outlining the dark parts with a very fine paintbrush. When it comes to giving the hair its shape, I use the airbrush. I cover up the rest of the picture with a loose, slightly raised mask, to achieve finer contours. Finally, I wash out some of the lighter portions with the paint-brush again and add the highlights – also with the paint-brush.

METTE: I'm sure quite a few of our readers will appreciate and enjoy these suggestions. One final point: Can you tell us very briefly how you see the future of the airbrush? And what advice can you give those who want to use it?

RÖSELER: I'm sure that in spite of computers the airbrush will continue to be a tool used for illustrations, though it may not remain quite as important as it is at the moment. My advice is that airbrush artists should put the greatest emphasis on drawing and composition skills and only use the airbrush as an aid, to help with their ideas.

METTE: Thank you very much indeed.

Left: "Deutschlandschaft" (German-scape)
Intended use: entry for competition
Format: 70 x 50 cm
Ground: illustration line board
Colours: Schmincke gouache
Airbrush: Grafo SP

Below: "Sea Woman"
Format: 70 x 50 cm
Ground: illustration line board
Colours: Schmincke gouache
Airbrush: Grafo SP

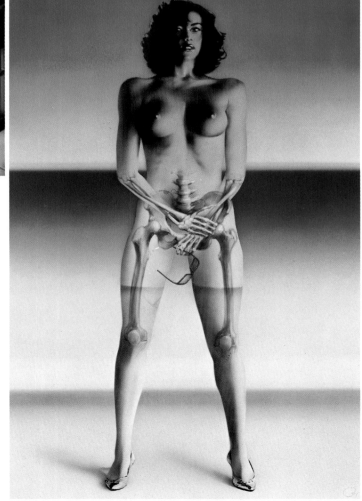

PETER RÖSELER

Below: "The Breakdown"
Intended use: magazine illustration
Format: 50 x 70 cm
Ground: illustration line board
Colours: Schmincke gouache
Airbrush: Grafo SP
Commissioned by: Penthouse competition

Top right: "Emancipation 1"
Intended use: magazine illustration
Format: 70 x 50 cm
Ground: illustration line board
Colours: Schmincke gouache
Airbrush: Grafo SP

Bottom right: "Death Valley"
Intended use: record sleeve
Format: 50 x 70 cm
Ground: illustration line board
Colours: Schmincke gouache
Airbrush: Grafo SP

Left: "Marilyn"
Intended use: magazine illustration
Format: 50 x 70 cm
Ground: illustration line board
Colours: Schmincke gouache
Airbrush: Grafo SP

Right: "Henry M"
Intended use: self–promotion
Format: 70 x 50 cm
Ground: illustration line board
Colours: Schmincke gouache
Airbrush: Grafo SP

Below: "Model B"
Intended use: self-promotion
Format: 70 x 50 cm
Ground: illustration line board
Colours: Schmincke gouache
Airbrush: Grafo SP

Far left: Untitled
Intended use: video cover
Format: 70 x 50 cm
Ground: illustration line board
Colours: Schmincke gouache
Airbrush: Grafo SP

Left: "Parrot"
Intended use: magazine illustration
Format: 70 x 50 cm
Ground: illustration line board
Colours: Schmincke gouache
Airbrush: Grafo SP

Bottom left: "Rockets"
Intended use: magazine illustration
Format: 60 x 70 cm
Ground: illustration line board
Colours: Schmincke gouache
Airbrush: Grafo SP

Bottom right: "Served Hot"
Intended use: exhibition poster
Format: 50 x 60 cm
Ground: illustration line board
Colours: Schmincke gouache
Airbrush: Grafo SP

LOTHAR STEDTLER comes from Overath near Cologne and is an old hand. He specializes in medical and technical illustrations.

METTE: You do some of your illustrations on photographic paper. Why?

STEDTLER: I started off using photos as my basis and then I worked with them. Nowadays I only use photographic paper if the surface has to be extremely smooth, and this is really only the case with simple, large areas. As soon as a job is more complicated, I prefer a different ground.

METTE: Why's that? Surely it's a good thing for the paint to be applied evenly, isn't it?

STEDTLER: I use mainly Tempera and Aerocolor. If you spray Aerocolor or similar paints straight onto photographic paper and you have to mask it up again, it can happen that the colour particles peel off with the masking film. Only glaze is safe enough not to damage double-masked areas of colour – but I don't find it opaque enough.

That's why I prefer working with 250-gramme hard board, because it minimizes the problem a little. Unless, of course, you re-mask too quickly, i.e. when the paint is still wet.

METTE: What do you actually do when you've made a mistake?

STEDTLER: Fortunately I know the technical possibilities of modern lithography. I usually mend things with opaque colours. The camera doesn't register these mistakes any longer. Occasionally there may be a slight problem with reproduction if there are white or very light pastel shades. But once you know about this problem, you can usually avoid it.

If the original itself has to be displayed and an impeccable picture is therefore required, I usually have to make a fresh start after a mistake.

METTE: Which airbrushes do you use?

STEDTLER: I've got three EFBE airbrushes. The EFBE is a good quality single-action airbrush, which I've known for over 30 years now. I first came across it when I was training and it's the one I like best. I never used to be able to cope with the other type, the double-action one.

Later, in the fifties, I illustrated shoes for an advertising agency called McCann's, together with a retoucher. We used to paint the shoes in their original sizes, i.e. about two inches. That's where I learnt to be 'pernickety'. And my EFBE really did a good job there.

Then I forgot all about the airbrush for a few years. During that time I was working for two advertising agencies, one after another, as an art director. This was mainly fashion and trade-fair work.

METTE: Well, as far as I know, you're self-employed now. How did you get onto that?

STEDTLER: I was already 52 years old. I had reached the upper limit at the agency, as far as promotion prospects were concerned. I just happened to come across a new agency which drew entirely on freelance illustrators. For about six months I tried working for them at the same time as I was doing my own job and in 1978 decided to go independent.

I just took the plunge. But like most creative artists, I was happy to take risks. And I haven't regretted this step ever since. If someone like myself has been doing this job right from the beginning and knows all the ins and outs, there isn't really that much of a risk in it.

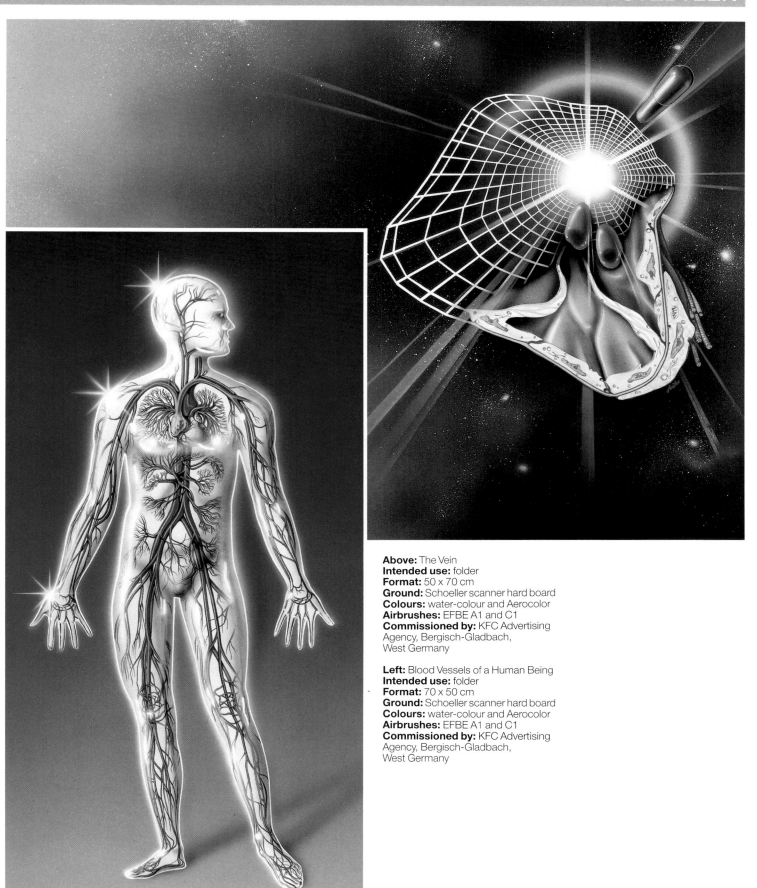

Above: The Vein
Intended use: folder
Format: 50 x 70 cm
Ground: Schoeller scanner hard board
Colours: water-colour and Aerocolor
Airbrushes: EFBE A1 and C1
Commissioned by: KFC Advertising
Agency, Bergisch-Gladbach,
West Germany

Left: Blood Vessels of a Human Being
Intended use: folder
Format: 70 x 50 cm
Ground: Schoeller scanner hard board
Colours: water-colour and Aerocolor
Airbrushes: EFBE A1 and C1
Commissioned by: KFC Advertising
Agency, Bergisch-Gladbach,
West Germany

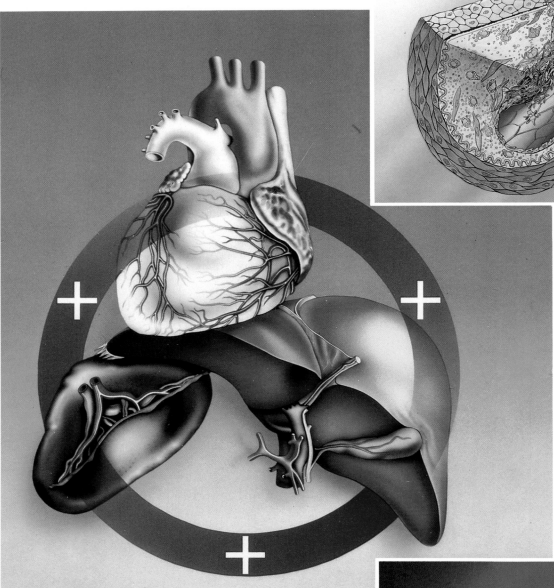

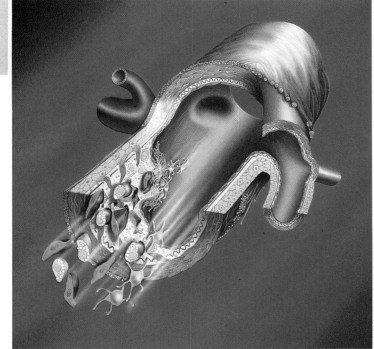

Above: Blocked Artery
Intended use: brochure for patients
Format: 40 x 50 cm
Ground: Schoeller scanner hard board
Colours: Aerocolor
Airbrush: Fischer Set G1 83
Commissioned by: PB Advertising
Agency, Cologne

Above: Heart – Liver – Spleen
Intended use: poster
Format: 100 x 70 cm
Ground: Schoeller Parole smooth
Colours: Designers gouache and
Magic Color
Airbrushes: EFBE A1 and C1
Commissioned by: PB Advertising
Agency, Cologne

Right: Unblocking of an Artery
Intended use: brochure for patients
Format: 100 x 70 cm
Ground: Schoeller Parole smooth
Colours: Designers gouache and
Magic Color
Airbrushes: EFBE A1 and C1
Commissioned by: PB Advertising
Agency, Cologne

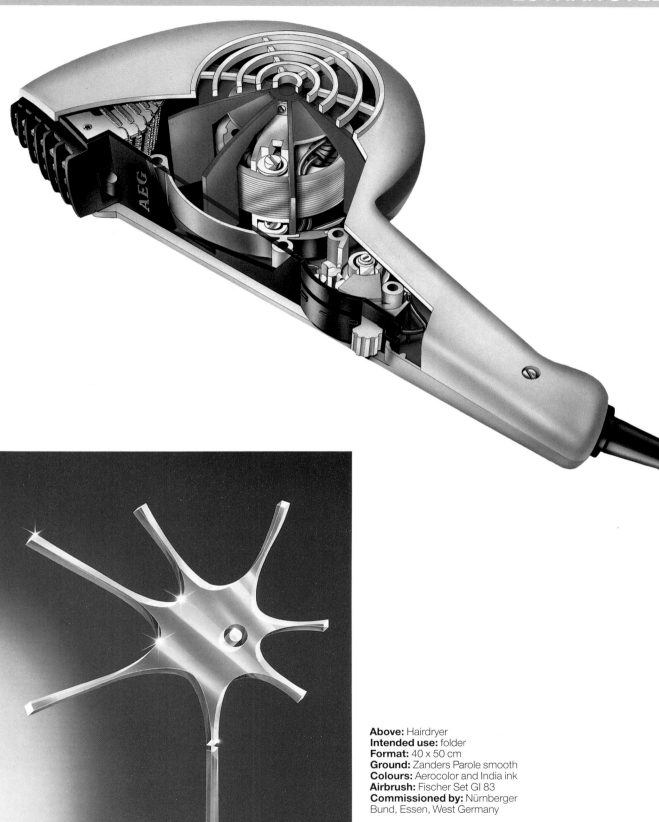

Above: Hairdryer
Intended use: folder
Format: 40 x 50 cm
Ground: Zanders Parole smooth
Colours: Aerocolor and India ink
Airbrush: Fischer Set GI 83
Commissioned by: Nürnberger
Bund, Essen, West Germany

Left: Nerve Cell
Intended use: symbol for
advertisements and folder
Format: 50 x 40 cm
Ground: Zanders Parole smooth
Colours: Designers gouache
Airbrush: EFBE A1 and C1
Commissioned by: PB Advertising
Agency, Cologne

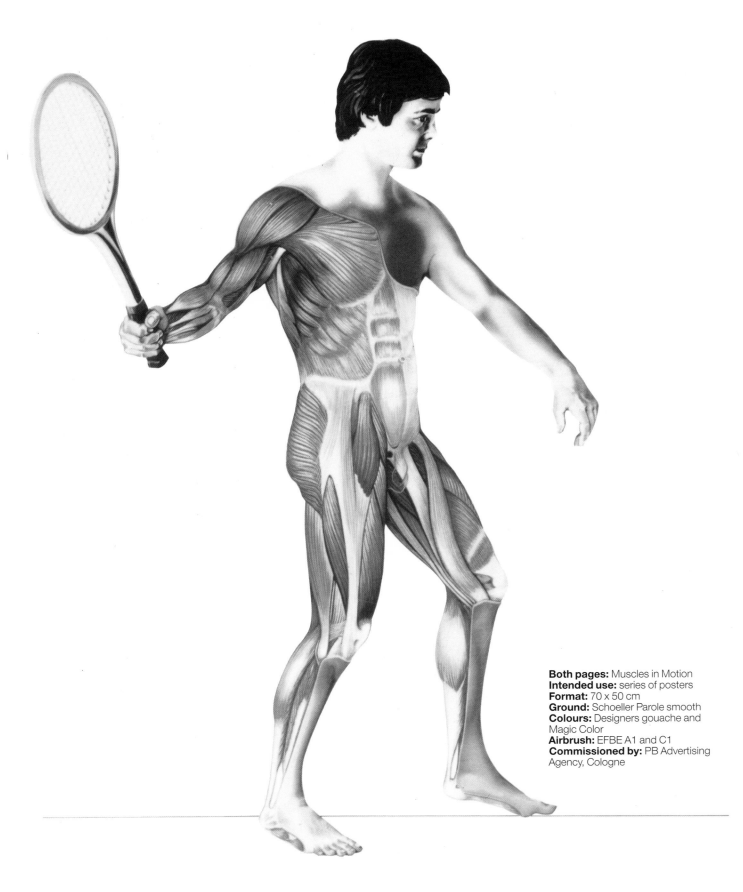

Both pages: Muscles in Motion
Intended use: series of posters
Format: 70 x 50 cm
Ground: Schoeller Parole smooth
Colours: Designers gouache and Magic Color
Airbrush: EFBE A1 and C1
Commissioned by: PB Advertising Agency, Cologne

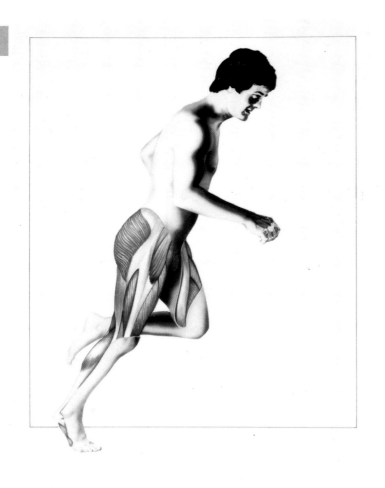

TECHNICAL ART, the name of LUDWIG EBERL and NORBERT SCHÄFER's firm, is also the designation of the whole genre that they represent. Technical art does not just come from Japan and Britain, but also from Germany.

LUDWIG EBERL (born 1929) and NORBERT SCHÄFER (born 1940) have been working together for over twenty years and they also like the same kind of subjects. One has to be mad about cars to create works like the ones shown on the following pages.

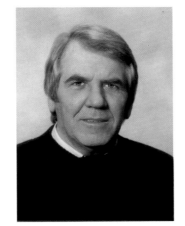
Ludwig Eberl

Both artists had originally trained as retouchers of positives. Both started their career at the art colleges in Offenbach and Stuttgart. After several jobs in different firms, they met for the first time in 1965 – and they have been working together ever since.

In 1976 they started their own company, called TECHNICAL ART. Under this name their illustrations became famous all over the world.

When I visited their studio in Dietzenbach near Frankfurt and had the opportunity to take a good look at their originals for the first time, I was quite impressed. It does not often happen that you come across so much perfection in the minutest of details.

So let us see what NORBERT SCHÄFER himself says about this particular aspect of his work, as well as several other topics.

NORBERT SCHÄFER: Well, you see, these works are the result of years of experience. For the beginner they should really only be something to help them aim in the right direction. One should not make the mistake of expecting too much of oneself while one is still on the way towards that long-term objective called perfection.

Norbert Schäfer

I've come quite a long way, too. It took me lots of steps to reach the point where I am now, so many stages in fact that if I had set my aims too high at the beginning, I would have got frustrated very quickly. I wouldn't have been able to reach them right at the beginning anyway.

Looking back, I would say that I've spent the last ten or fifteen years learning new things all the time. It's been exactly the same for my partner, LUDWIG EBERL. It certainly took us quite a while to get to that point.

Lots of my pictures would have looked different ten years ago.

METTE: How do you get all the information for these pictures? I suppose you're given technical drawings by your clients, aren't you?

SCHÄFER: That's right.

METTE: And you do the actual constructing yourselves, i.e. the perspective drawings?

SCHÄFER: Yes. Well, not always, but most of the time, of course. Sometimes a lot of good preliminary work has been done by the manufacturer himself. When we painted the camera, we were given the original as a model. But we were also given another model that was cut open so that we could see the inside.

The idea was that we should get a precise idea of the material and also the technology. Although a purely technical drawing would have shown every single detail, there would have been so many overlaps in it that we'd have had to work with an enormous number of detailed drawings. Theoretically, of course, you can do anything. The question is only whether it can be put into practice or not. And there are cases where it is sensible to cut open an original model so that you can be more confident when you're doing the actual work. The time factor is often more important than the cost of a damaged model.

The work itself is still difficult enough as it is.

METTE: I could imagine that there are times when the information which you get from your client isn't quite sufficient for the work you're doing. If that is the case, how do you fill the gaps? Do you ever go to a technical museum?

SCHÄFER: We do indeed. BMW, for instance, has an automobile museum. When we were working for them, we used to go there occasionally to find out about various things.

METTE: Do you always work on this thick, laminated hard board or do you sometimes used scanner-friendly 250-gramme hard board.

SCHÄFER: We only use the thick variety. The most important thing for us is to have a firm base, a firm ground for our work. Everything else comes second.

If an illustration needs to be reproduced, we just have slides made.

METTE: I noticed that you always put some interesting highlights onto your pictures.

SCHÄFER: We do that quite deliberately. The subject of technology is dry enough as it is. We try to put a bit more dynamism and depth into our pictures by the way we distribute light and darkness. And sometimes we put in light and colour effects, even though – from a technological point of view – there's no reason for this at all. But we think this is quite a legitimate way of improving the mood of a picture, its general impression.

METTE: How long does it take you to paint a picture like that of the BMW racing car?

SCHÄFER: Well, I suppose you can reckon between two hundred and two hundred and fifty hours. There are times, though, when there is a limit to the amount of time we can put into a picture.

METTE: How come your clients want to go to such lengths? In other words, what do they do with your illustrations?

SCHÄFER: Mostly they use them for advertising: single ads, brochures and also for trade-fair exhibitions. But it also happens quite frequently that the illustrations are used for magazine articles. Nearly all the professional journals have used our illustrations at some stage.

METTE: I remember some time ago I came across some artistic reprints of the motorbikes you painted. Do you ever do such jobs just for the fun of it?

SCHÄFER: That was in fact a whole series. We wanted to show motorbikes not just from a technical point of view but also in an interesting context.

There were three models which we printed in nine colours, very expensively and in a limited edition, and then put on the market.

We just wanted to explore a different path, other than taking on commissioned work and writing an invoice – none of that. We simply wanted to work more freely. Later, we made posters of our pictures or had them made.

METTE: Can I just very quickly ask you a question about a completely different topic? Are there any particular types of paints you prefer?

SCHÄFER: We used to work mainly with tempera. But that has changed. Nowadays we use acrylic a lot more, although we still use tempera occasionally. With our technique we just find it easier to use opaque colours.

METTE: A final request: can you tell us which stages you went through when you made one of these car pictures?

SCHÄFER: It's really always the same with all pictures. We start by getting hold of all the reference material. This means taking a lot of photos, of the whole car itself and also of the most important technical details. And of course we also need the technical drawings, if there are any.

This has to be done secretly sometimes because we often get such jobs before the vehicles have been put on the market.

Once we've got everything, we can start making our own drawings. We plan the entire illustration on tracing paper. All the details that can be seen, say, when a model is cut open, must be fixed quite accurately at this stage.

And before we start on our final illustration, we need to have discussed everything with our client. If at all possible, there should not be any technical errors at this stage, because it would take hours to mend them afterwards.

This basic drawing is then transferred onto the ground. This is the point where colour comes into it. Areas and contours are sprayed, and the smaller and tiniest details are painted with a paintbrush. That's all really.

METTE: Seems as if the last stage is quite easy, in fact. Thank you very much indeed.

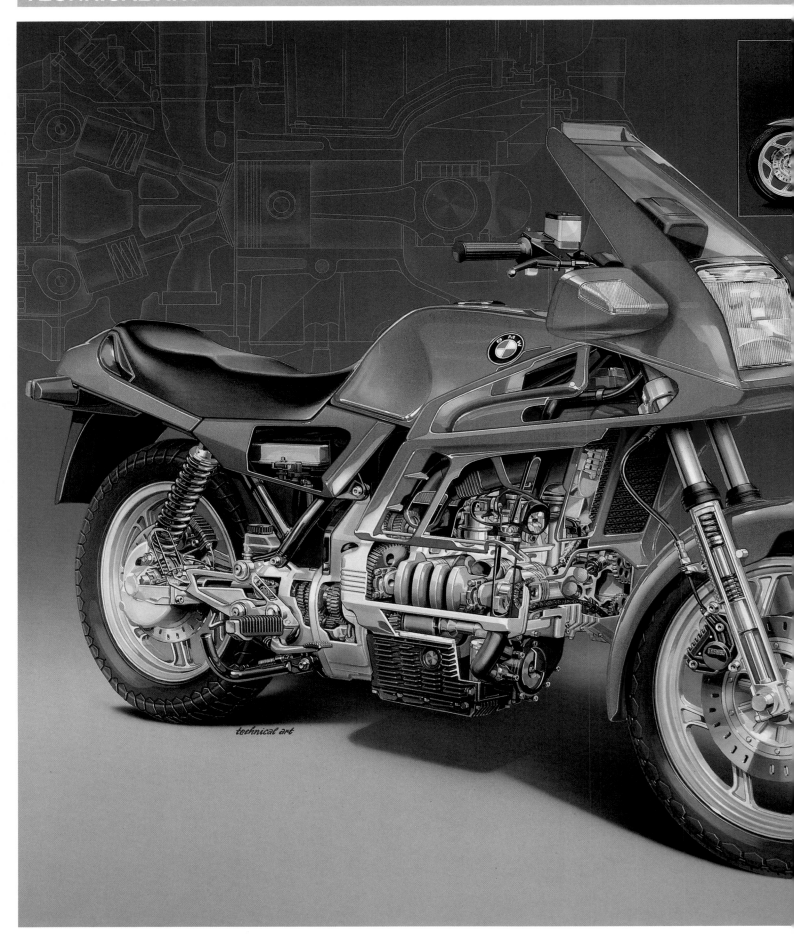

technical art

Above: Opel Diesel engine 1.6 litres
Intended use: brochures, trade-fair poster
Format: 50 x 60 cm
Ground: illustration line board
Colours: Schmincke gouache
Airbrush: Grafo
Commissioned by: McCann-Erickson GmbH

Left: BMW K 100 RS
Format: 60 x 70 cm
Ground: illustration line board
Colours: Schmincke gouache and Liquitex
Airbrush: Grafo
Commissioned by: BMW Motorrad GmbH

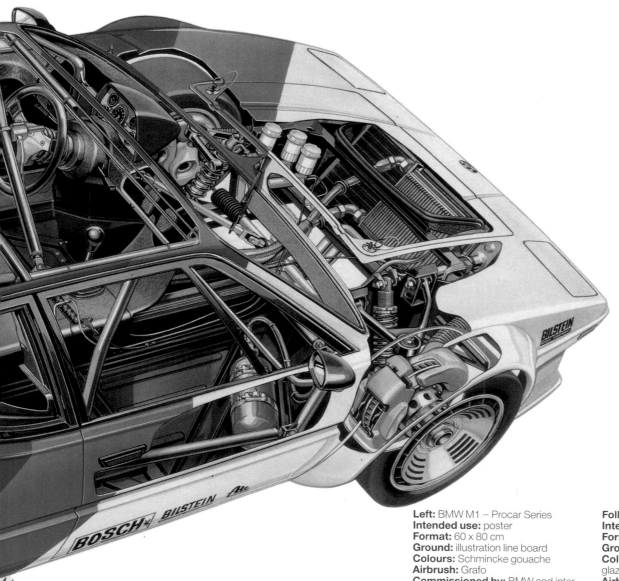

Left: BMW M1 – Procar Series
Intended use: poster
Format: 60 x 80 cm
Ground: illustration line board
Colours: Schmincke gouache
Airbrush: Grafo
Commissioned by: BMW and international motoring magazines

Following pages: Krupp crane truck
Intended use: technical illustration
Format: 45 x 45 cm
Ground: illustration line board
Colours: Schmincke gouache and glaze
Airbrush: Grafo
Commissioned by: Krupp, Wilhelmshaven, West Germany

TECHNICAL ART

Right: Suzuki Katana
Intended use: art prints
Format: 50 x 60 cm
Ground: illustration line board
Colours: Schmincke gouache and
Liquitex
Airbrush: Grafo

Left: BMW Series 3
Intended use: Poster
Format: 60 x 80 cm
Ground: illustration line board
Colours: Schmincke gouache
Airbrush: Grafo
Commissioned by: BMW and inter-
national motoring magazines

Right: Leica M 6
Intended use: brochure and other
advertising media
Format: 40 x 50 cm
Ground: illustration line board
Colours: Schmincke gouache
Airbrush: Grafo
Commissioned by: Ernst Leitz
Wetzlar GmbH

GETTING any information about Klaus Wagger from Bad Häring in Austria was the most difficult job of all. When I first tried to ring him, he was not at home but travelling around somewhere in Australia.

But he obviously has a very efficient PR manager, i.e. his own family. I told them on the telephone that I wanted to write a book and would like to include KLAUS WAGGER, and lo and behold: a week later there was a letter from Melbourne on my desk.

The reason why I had decided to include a section on KLAUS WAGGER was because I rather liked his

work. I must say, though, that I had already met him personally at an informal airbrushers' meeting in a pub in Munich, where he made a good impression on me. He put forward a few very firm, mature views with regard to illustrations in general and the airbrush in particular.

KLAUS WAGGER is one of the youngest of illustrators and can be expected to leave his mark on the airbrush scene in future. He was born in Tyrol in 1959, went to primary school and grammar school and then studied industrial design at Linz. This course took five years. One of his ideas, which he put forward at our meeting in Munich, is expressed very clearly in his letter, namely

that he never wants to lose his independence. This is why, after college, he did not want to tread the well-worn path of joining a studio or an agency, looking for a more pleasant way of making a living.

In winter he began to work as a skiing instructor in his native Austria, and in summer he built surf boards. The latter is also the reason why he prefers large formats.

While he was working on surf boards, he came across the airbrush for the first time. He carried on with this job until the end of 1983.

Although he did not actually join the Establishment from that point onwards, he did begin to concentrate mainly on illustrations. He himself feels that there has been a tendency towards technical drawing in his work, particularly in his more recent pictures. It is something which he is good at and which he enjoys. Hardly surprising, considering that he has a degree in industrial design.

I would like to conclude this section with KLAUS WAGGER's own words, which I think are quite typical of him:

"Under no circumstances would I want to cut out independent work. It is by far the most important thing for my mental well-being."

KLAUS WAGGER

Right: "Once Upon A Time ..."
Intended use: Poster
Format: 90 x 60 cm
Ground: Schoellershammer 4 G thick
Colours: Aerocolor and Magic Color
Airbrushes: Iwata HP-A and
Paasche V1
Commissioned by: Verkerke

Below: "Jags"
Intended use: Poster
Format: 70 x 100 cm
Ground: Schoellershammer 4 G thick
Colours: Aerocolor
Airbrush: Iwata HP-A

156

Left: "Panthers Go Downtown"
Intended use: Poster
Format: 85 x 60 cm
Ground: Schoellershammer 4 G thick
Colours: Aerocolor
Airbrushes: Iwata HP-A and
Paasche V1

Below: "Porsche 911"
Intended use: technical illustration
Format: 50 x 70 cm
Ground: Schoellershammer 4 G thick
Colours: Magic Color
Airbrush: Paasche V1

Above: "Crusin' Missile '59"
Intended use: poster
Format: 70 x 100 cm
Ground: Schoellershammer 4 G thick
Colours: Aerocolor and India ink
Airbrushes: Iwata HP-A and
Paasche V1

Left: "Yamaha XT 550"
Intended use: technical illustration
Format: 50 x 40 cm
Ground: Schoellershammer 4 G thick
Colours: Aerocolor
Airbrush: Iwata HP-A

Left: Untitled
Intended use: poster
Format: 80 x 50 cm
Ground: Schoellershammer 4 G thick
Colours: Aerocolor and gouache
Airbrush: Iwata HP-A

Right: "Crush-Proof"
Intended use: poster
Format: 70 x 100 cm
Ground: Schoellershammer 4 G thick
Colours: Magic Color and Prismacolor
coloured pencils
Airbrush: Paasche V1

159

Left: Untitled
Intended use: poster
Format: 75 x 60 cm
Ground: Schoellershammer 4 G thick
Colours: Aerocolor and Gouache
Airbrush: Iwata HP-A

Below: "Splash"
Format: 70 x 100 cm
Ground: Schoellershammer 4 G thick
Colours: Aerocolor
Airbrushes: Iwata HP-A and
Paasche V1

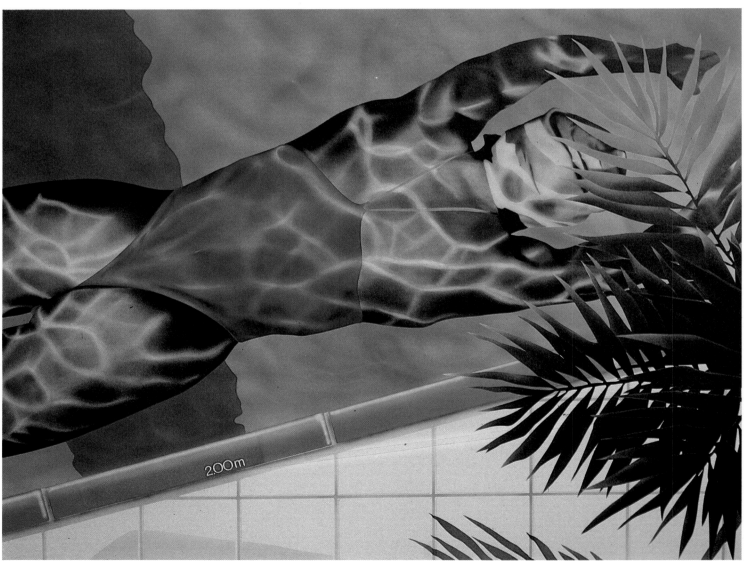

MAL is short for Malcolm and he lives in Yorkshire but his pictures have become world-famous by now. He has his home in Harrogate, a nice old Victorian town north of Leeds. He has even been introduced in a newspaper as being Harrogate's best-known contemporary artist.

MAL WATSON was born in 1953 and comes from a working-class family, which may explain the stamina and perseverance he has displayed in his career. His life has been anything but conventional, though by no means unusual among artists of a similar kind.

He left school without O levels at the age of 15 and spent the next seven years rather aimlessly doing all kinds of odd jobs. He himself admits that he did not have any precise future plans at that stage.

It was not until 1975 that he decided to do a two-year course at a local college of art. However, after only a year he broke it off again. This is what he says about his experiences at that time:

"There was too much emphasis on theory and very little practical work. As far as I'm concerned, the only positive thing during those twelve months was my first contact with the airbrush.

So I decided to stand on my own legs again and spent all my savings, £400 at the time, on my first airbrush and a compressor."

The next few years were a hard slog and MAL WATSON developed a kind of love-hate relationship with his airbrush. Following the trial-and-error principle he spent eighteen months experimenting with all the colours and grounds that he could get hold of.

What made life difficult for him at the time was the lack of reading material on airbrush technique, for even in England the airbrush was virtually unheard-of for a long time. This has of course changed considerably since then.

MALS's debut as a commercial illustrator consisted of a series of richly coloured, abstract pictures which were bought by a chain of boutiques. That was not the breakthrough, though, which he had been hoping for.

"Although I had managed to sell my first pictures, I still had to fight for every single job, so I accepted everything I could get and lived on baked beans and toast.

I didn't become a real professional until July 1982. I had been looking for a representative for me and my work and then found one in my native Harrogate of all places. I have never regretted my decision since then."

The commissions began to pile up. MAL WATSON's illustrations were particularly popular with postcard and poster manufacturers. Most big companies in this large industry began to make use of the fairly decorative illustrations of this young Yorkshireman. And eventually he even managed to break through into the American market.

161

miniscence of the Golden Twenties and Thirties. He had a special reason for painting them:

"I wanted to show a touch of decadence. All airbrush illustrations are somehow similar, but in these works I tried to develop my own style.

However, I've still got both my legs firmly on the ground. All my work is commercially oriented. Many artists are a bit naïve when it comes to figures. But I am trying to be not only a good illustrator but also a successful businessman. I've always managed so far."

This marked sense of realism may well be partly due to his Yorkshire background.

Mal freely admits that he has been developing a preference for the States:

"I've been influenced quite a lot by American illustrators, and so has my style. I particularly like the so-called 'West Coast way of life' with its recurring motifs of beaches and big, fast cars.

I've subscribed to a good dozen or more American journals and magazines so that I can always have my finger on the pulse of our time. I might even get a double page in Playboy or a Bowie cover out of it one day."

The illustrations on the following pages include pictures by MAL WATSON which were painted as a re-

Above: "Bad Girls"
Intended use: poster
Format: 49 x 84 cm
Ground: Schoellershammer 4 G thick
Colours: Rotring Artist Color
Airbrush: Olympos Special SP-B
Commissioned by: Athena
International

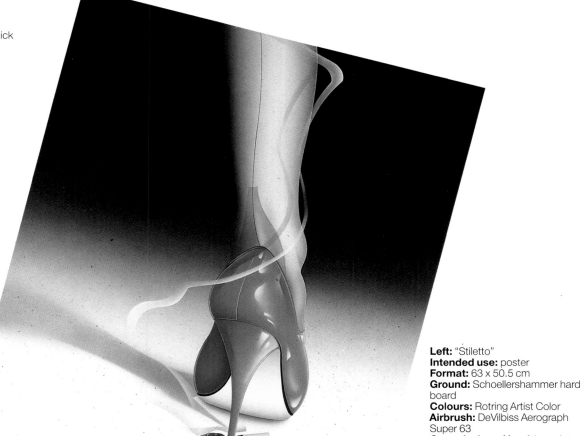

Left: "Stiletto"
Intended use: poster
Format: 63 x 50.5 cm
Ground: Schoellershammer hard
board
Colours: Rotring Artist Color
Airbrush: DeVilbiss Aerograph
Super 63
Commissioned by: Athena Inter-
national

Far left, top left: "High Society"
Intended use: art print
Format: 37 x 33.5 cm
Ground: Schoellershammer hard board
Colours: Rotring Artist Color and Pelikan India ink
Airbrush: DeVilbis Aerograph Super 63
Commissioned by: Athena International

Far left, top right: "Stripes"
Intended use: greetings card
Format: 37 x 28 cm
Ground: Schoellershammer hard board
Colours: Rotring Artist Color
Airbrush: DeVilbis Aerograph Super 63
Commissioned by: Beechwood Publications

Far left, bottom: "Music Lover"
Intended use: poster
Format: 61 x 81 cm
Ground: Schoellershammer hard board
Colours: Rotring Artist Color and Pelikan India ink
Airbrush: DeVilbis Aerograph Super 63
Commissioned by: Athena International, unpublished

Left: "Rare Deal"
Intended use: studio print
Format: 39 x 28 cm
Ground: Schoellershammer hard board
Colours: Rotring Artist Color
Airbrush: DeVilbis Aerograph Super 63
Commissioned by: Athena International

Below: "Switched On"
Intended use: greetings card
Format: 34 x 58 cm
Ground: Schoellershammer hard board
Colours: Magic Color
Airbrush: DeVilbis Aerograph Super 63
Commissioned by: Athena International

MAL WATSON/ORIENTAL LADY

Left: "Oriental Lady"
Intended use: art print
Format: 48 x 64 cm
Ground: Schoellershammer hard board
Colours: Magic Color
Airbrush: DeVilbiss Aerograph Super 63
Commissioned by: Athena International

Below: "Fast Lady 2"
Intended use: poster
Format: 61 x 88.5 cm
Ground: Schoellershammer hard board
Colours: Magic Color und Pelikan India ink
Airbrush: Olympos Special SP-B
Commissioned by: Athena International

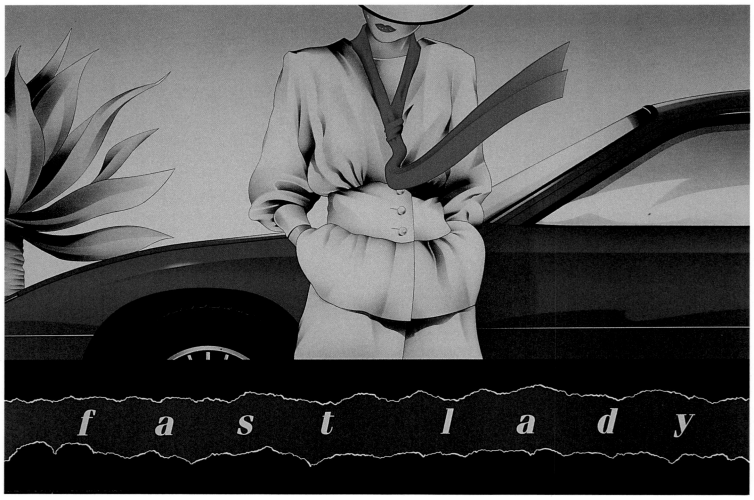

fast lady

Left: "Ferrari"
Intended use: poster
Format: 63 x 35 cm
Ground: Schoellershammer hard board
Colours: Magic Color und Pelikan India ink
Airbrush: Olympos Special SP-B
Commissioned by: Scandecor, Sweden

Below: "Fast Lady 1"
Intended use: poster
Format: 61 x 88.5 cm
Ground: Schoellershammer hard board
Colours: Magic Color und Pelikan India ink
Airbrush: Olympos Special SP-B
Commissioned by: Athena International

MAL WATSON

Right: "Top Hat"
Intended use: greetings card
Format: 47 x 34 cm
Ground: Schoellershammer hard board
Colours: Magic Color and Pelikan water-colour
Airbrush: DeVilbis Aerograph Super 63
Commissioned by: Celebration Arts, U.K.

Below: "Travel"
Intended use: poster
Format: 59.5 x 76 cm
Ground: CS 10 Line Board
Colours: Rotring Artist Color
Airbrush: Olympos Special SP-B
Commissioned by: Athena International